THE DIRECTOR
KNO

# JOHN SHAW
## ILLUSTRATED BY JOHN FOWLER

# THE **DIRECTORY** OF
# KNOTS

Grange BOOKS

First published in the UK in 2004 for Grange Books
an imprint of Grange Books plc
The Grange
Kingsnorth Industrial Estate
Hoo, nr Rochester
Kent ME3 9ND
www.Grangebooks.co.uk

By arrangement with THE IVY PRESS LIMITED

ISBN: 1-84013-663-4

Publisher's note
This book is a general introduction to the usefulness and
pleasure of knotting. Before using any one of these knots, bends,
hitches, etc. in a potentially hazardous situation—whether at work
or at leisure—with foreseeable risks of injury, damage, or loss, you are
strongly advised to seek the advice and tuition of suitably qualified
practitioners to learn how to tie and deploy
them in such a situation.

This book was conceived, designed, and produced by
THE IVY PRESS LIMITED
The Old Candlemakers, West Street, Lewes, East Sussex, BN7 2NZ

Creative Director *Peter Bridgewater*
Publisher *Sophie Collins*
Editorial Director *Steve Luck*
Design Manager *Tony Seddon*
Designer *Tonwen Jones*
Illustrator *John Fowler*
Project Editor *Mandy Greenfield*

Originated and printed in China

# CONTENTS

# INTRODUCTION

Anyone can tie a knot or two . . . or the 100 (and more)
contained in this book. If you cannot, it is merely
because you have not yet learned to do so. For knotting
is one of those basic skills, like the ability to swim or
read a map, that is accessible to all who choose to
acquire them and separates self-sufficient and confident
folk from the rest.

Tying knots is as satisfying as any other aspect of mental
and manual dexterity, but has practical applications.
In a new millennium that is likely to prove at least as
hostile to humankind as the last one, knot tyers are
among those helping to conserve the planet's dwindling
and finite resources; for knots are reusable and, unlike
factory-made and store-bought clips, clamps, and other
gadgets, come virtually free in terms of cash and energy
consumption. And knot tying can be fun.

Today's knotting exponents—liberated from the survival
needs for which our primitive ancestors first invented
knots (to snare food, tote loads, erect shelters, tether

animals, and bind or even strangle enemies)—are free to indulge in a wider-ranging exploration of the fundamental but fascinating art, craft, and science of knotting. For mathematicians there is the esoteric but rapidly growing postgraduate study of multidimensional knot theory; and, while there is no Nobel Prize for math, its equivalent (the Field's Medal) was awarded in 1990 to the New Zealander Professor Vaughan Jones, F.R.S., for original contributions to this arcane subject.

Anglers, astronauts, cavers and climbers, conjurors, trappers, tree surgeons, and wind surfers all know and use knots. They even invent new ones (some of which appear in this book). But you do not have to be an adventurous outdoor type, or a practitioner of some specialized skill, in order to benefit from knowing how to tie knots. You do not even have to like messing about in boats. Most knots are in fact tied by landlubbers, whether for leisure or for gain in cash and confidence, who find it an absorbing pursuit.

# Helpful terms

Learning to tie knots and then practicing them can be done with a variety of stuff—which is the common term used by knot tyers for cordage of all kinds (thin stuff, thick stuff, expensive stuff, et cetera). More precisely, anything over about ⅜ inch (10 mm) in diameter is called a rope, while lesser diameters may be termed braided cord, string, or twine, according to their size, construction, and quality.

Rope that consists of three strands is known as a hawser, but a rope that is made up of a number of filaments enclosed in a braided outer covering is (depending on the way it is made) said to be sheath-&-core (kernmantel, in the case of climbing ropes) or braid-on-braid construction. Any rope or cord with a specific use is a line (for example, a towline, a washing line, a heaving or throwing line).

Cordage manufactured in the age-old way from the fibrous stems, leaves, and seeds of plants includes coir, cotton, flax, hemp, and jute. The latest products, however, comprise synthetic monofilaments and multifilaments that have been obtained mainly from the four Ps: polyamide (nylon), polyester (terylene or dacron), polypropylene, and polyethylene (polythene). These durable manmade products are augmented by several so-called "super or miracle fibers," such as Kevlar, which are marketed under various trade names.

The stuff that is sold in stores selling household goods will be cheaper by as much as a factor of 10 than the high-tech cordage stocked by ship chandlers or by climbing and camping suppliers. Indeed, because cordage can be costly, cut ends should always be heat-sealed, taped, or seized with a length of thin twine to prevent waste from needless fraying or unraveling. However, all that is required to learn and practice the knots described in this book are two 6-foot (2-m) lengths of flexible, braided cord about ⅓ inch (8 mm) in diameter, preferably in two different colors so that the separate routes may be followed when tying two different lines together.

In all of the tying instructions that follow, the end that is actively involved in the tying process is referred to as the *working end*. The other end is known as the *standing end*, while that part of the rope or cord in between is known as the *standing part*. Any well defined U-shape within this standing part is called a *bight*, and a bight may also be made by doubling over the working end.

Once a bight acquires a *crossing point* it becomes a *loop*, and a couple of closely linked crossing points form *elbows*. A loop may be either overhand (when the working end is laid on top of the standing part) or underhand (when the working end is placed beneath the standing part). Knotted loops may be either fixed or adjustable (in other words, sliding), the latter commonly being called nooses. During the tying process some knots accumulate a series of unsecured knot parts resembling the rungs of a ladder. These must eventually be fixed in place by passing the working end between them, going alternately over, under, over, under; this is known as a *locking tuck*.

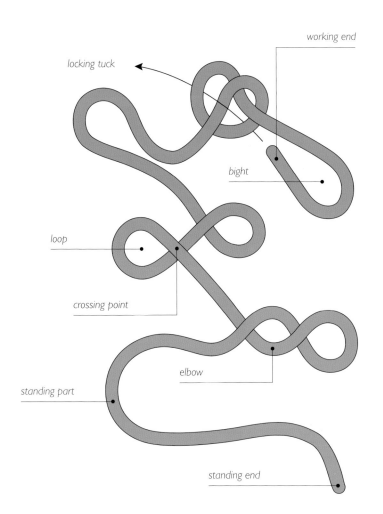

working end

locking tuck

bight

loop

crossing point

elbow

standing part

standing end

# ON KNOTS IN GENERAL

The generic name for any cordage tie is a "knot," but knots that join two lines together are identified as bends, while knots that attach a line to a rail, ring, post, or even another rope are known as hitches.

Strictly speaking, only something other than a bend or a hitch is a knot, including bindings, shortenings, stoppers, and loops. There are exceptions. For instance, many loops make useful hitches since they can be cast on, off, and on again, without the need to untie and retie them. And because earlier generations of seamen spoke of "bending" any line to a ring, some ring hitches are actually called bends. Then again, bends and hitches primarily tied in small stuff, such as fishing line or package twine, are only ever referred to as knots.

Knots are the tools that make rope and other cordage work to justify its initial cost. Fortunately many are extremely versatile, all-purpose contrivances. The same knot, bend, or hitch in rope might rescue someone from a mountain ledge or support a clothes line of freshly washed garments; yet, when tied in hair-thin nylon monofilament, it could be the means by which an angler lands a record-breaking fish. A stopper knot can prevent a rope block-&-tackle coming adrift or it can keep a sewing thread within the eye of a needle. It is just a matter of scale. Learn one knot, and you get at least another one free.

As a rule, knots weaken the cordage in which they occur. Knots tied quickly and simply are often the worst. Bulkier knots, with more wrapping turns, are stronger—that is, they reduce the breaking strength of line less drastically—but tying them may be trickier. So the selection of knot strength is a trade-off, a compromise between safety and convenience.

A knot may be strong, yet will slip and fall apart if tugged spasmodically or shaken, in which case it is insecure. Knot "security" is a separate consideration from knot "strength." A knot must be both strong and secure enough for the job in hand.

# SOME BASIC KNOTS

A few simple knots feature repeatedly on later pages of this book as component parts of other more elaborate knots, so they are introduced briefly here. The *overhand knot*, tied in the end of a rope or cord, is a basic stopper knot, an unsightly way of preventing the end of a length of line from fraying, but a useful means of stopping it pulling out of a hole or slot.

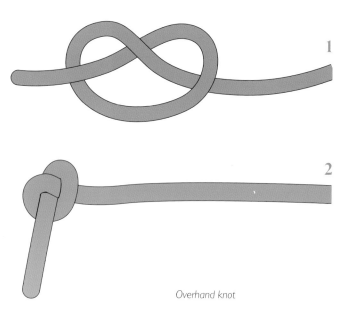

*Overhand knot*

The *figure-eight knot* is a better stopper knot than the overhand knot. Although it may appear to be bulkier, it does not actually have a greater diameter or block a bigger hole than the overhand knot. However, the figure-eight does having the advantage of being rather easier to untie after use, and is popular with knot-tyers because of its distinctive outline.

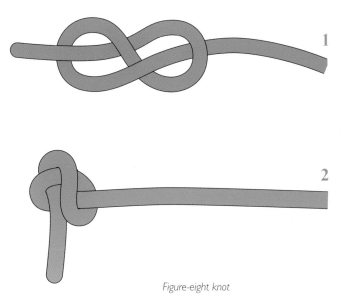

Figure-eight knot

When a drawloop (a bight made when the working end of the rope is not pulled completely through a knot) is added to the figure eight, it becomes a *slipped figure eight*. The drawloop ensures that the knot can always be untied by tugging on the working end. There is a case for using drawloops more frequently, since they do not weaken the knot—it is even possible that they may strengthen it.

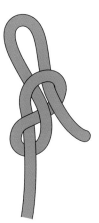

*Slipped figure eight*

When an overhand knot is rearranged around a rail, ring, rope, or spar, it becomes a *half hitch*. However, when it is tied in both ends of the same line as a binding around or against something, it is referred to as a *half knot*.

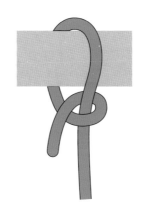

*Half hitch 1*

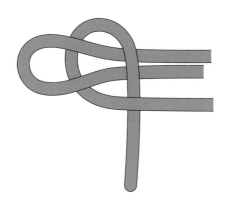

*Half hitch 2*

*Half knot*

Tuck the working end of an overhand knot a second time, pull gently on both ends to tighten it, and it twists and wraps around itself to create a *double overhand knot.*

Notice how the overhand, figure-eight, and double overhand knots all change their shape when tightened. Many other knots do. Be amenable when a knot tells you what it wants to do—it usually knows best.

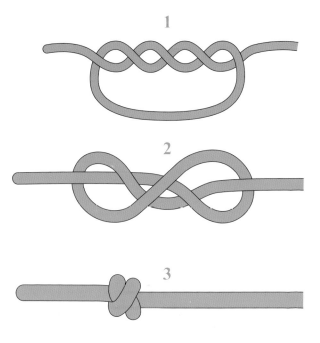

*Double overhand knot*

# THE WORLD'S FAVORITE KNOTS

*"Although there are thousands of different knots . . . there are a few knots which have proven their worth as the ones most generally useful."*

PERCY W. BLANDFORD, 1980

Watch those professionals who work with rope or smaller cordage and it soon becomes apparent that their knotting repertoire is restricted to a total of no more than perhaps ten knots, bends, and hitches. Almost certainly they know more, and may use them in certain situations, but they routinely rely on a selection of general-purpose and time-honored holdfasts.

# INTRODUCTION

There are sensible reasons why those who tie a lot of knots tend to restrict their fingers to the same few tried-and-trusted ones. The need for any knot can arise at short notice, when it must be applied immediately, without time to consider which of several other alternatives might be preferable. Tying the knot itself should be done quickly, implying a practiced familiarity with it. Then again, if the person who is tying the knot is one of a team or crew, it is essential that every member of that group can readily recognize and untie whatever has been previously applied by someone else. So the tyer must know that whatever he or she is tying will not later present the other members of the group with any sort of snag or difficulty.

Faced with the task of attaching a line to a rail, spar, or post, generations of rope-workers have settled on the simple clove hitch (which can be tied by several differing methods) and its close relative the rolling hitch; and, for a ring hitch, on the round turn & two half hitches or its reliable cousin, the fisherman's bend.

To tie a fixed loop into the end of a line, often as a substitute for a hitch, our knotting ancestors relied upon a common bowline and its tougher variants, the water bowline and the double (or round turn) bowline. A simple adaptation of one or another of these—into a running bowline—served them well enough as a sliding noose.

To join two lines together they chose a basic sheet bend or, for more demanding jobs, the one-way and the double sheet bends. Meanwhile, in smaller stuff, the tendency was to employ a fisherman's knot (single, double, or triple).

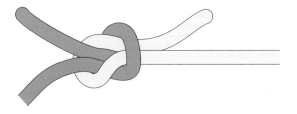

*Reef knot*

For odd jobs, a handy trio soon emerged: the reef knot, as a binding knot; the sheepshank, for a shortening; and the figure-eight stopper knot.

# FIGURE-EIGHT
# STOPPER KNOT

This knot is preferable to the overhand knot as a stopper, simply because it is easier to untie after use. Although bulkier, it will not fill a bigger hole. Tie it in the end of any rope that must remain within a pulley block or other item of rigging hardware.

Make a bight in the working end of the line and twist it around 180°, creating a loop (1).

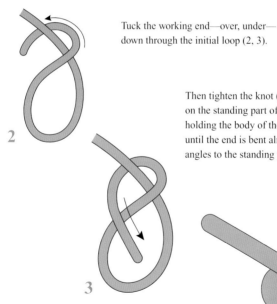

Tuck the working end—over, under—down through the initial loop (2, 3).

Then tighten the knot (4), pulling down on the standing part of the line while holding the body of the knot stationary, until the end is bent almost at right angles to the standing part of the line.

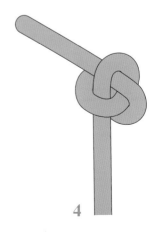

### ORIGIN
The nautical name for the figure-eight knot is Flemish knot, implying some kind of real or imagined western Germanic source.

# SHEEPSHANK
## TIED IN THE BIGHT

This oddly named knot is a basic shortening for a rope or cord that is too long for the job in hand, and too good to be cut to the required size. It works best with line that is hung vertically, because the knot (which is otherwise quite insecure) falls apart if no strain is placed upon it. Nevertheless it is a handy contrivance, readily tied in the bight.

Fold the spare standing part of the rope into three (making an S or Z shape), and slide an underhand loop over the upper bight (1, 2). This is sometimes known as a bellringer's knot, from its use in suspending surplus rope safely in a church belfry.

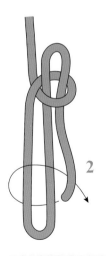

**1**

To complete the knot, add a similar half hitch to the lower bight (3).

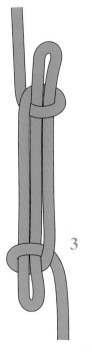

**2**

**3**

### ORIGIN

It is most unlikely this knot was ever used for tethering sheep so that they were restricted to grazing an area of grass defined by the length of the shortened rope that held them. The name is more likely to have come from the knot's resemblance to a sheep's legbone.

# SHEEPSHANK
## TIED WITH ENDS

The basic sheepshank tied in the bight (*see page 23*) is an insecure knot that falls apart if not steadily loaded. Rarely is a rope or cord so long that it must be made that way; and, when either or both ends are accessible, it is better to tie this wholly secure modification.

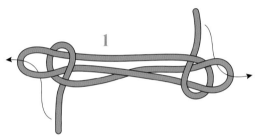

**1**

Tie a sheepshank in the bight and then simply tuck each end through its adjacent bight (1, 2).

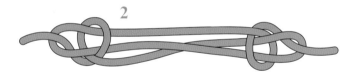

**2**

Tighten both resulting end knots, taking care to ensure that the trio of intervening strands are the same length and so will share any load equally between them (3).

**3**

# CLOVE HITCH
# TIED WITH AN END

This classic hitch can be rapidly applied and just as quickly taken apart again. It resembles a letter N (or its mirror-image, if the knot is tied the other way round). As long as the strain on it is more or less at right angles to the anchorage point, it will hold well enough; but it will loosen, slip, and may come adrift if pulled or tugged askew.

Take a turn with the working end around the rail, ring, rope, or spar, and then lay it diagonally over its own standing part (1, 2).

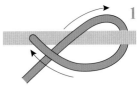

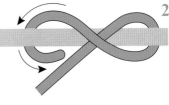

Pass the end around once more, and finally tuck the end beneath itself (3).

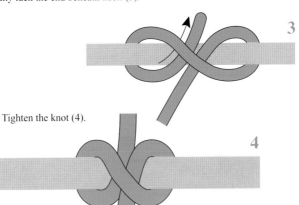

Tighten the knot (4).

## ORIGIN

Centuries ago this hitch was known as a builder's knot, a reminder that at least as many bends and hitches were tied ashore as they were aboard square-rigged ships. Its current name originated in *The Universal Dictionary of the Marine* (1769) by William Falconer.

# CLOVE HITCH TIED IN THE BIGHT

Tying any knot "in the bight" generally results in a more fluent manipulation, and this knot is no exception to the rule. In addition, it brings about dynamic control of whatever is loading the standing part of the line.

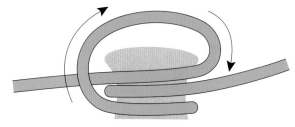

1

Cast an underhand loop (that is, one in which the line nearest the end goes beneath the standing part) and place it over the post, stanchion, tree stump, or whatever else is to be the anchorage point (1).

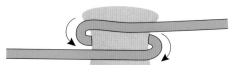

2

Use the friction generated by this turn to control, slow, and stop the load. Adjust the standing part to the required length and then add a second underhand loop to complete and secure the knot (2, 3).

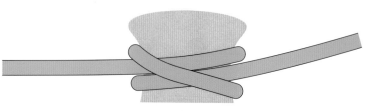

3

# ROLLING HITCH

Closely related to the clove hitch (*see pages 25 and 26*), this descendant evolved to cope with a longitudinal pull of any kind.

Pass the working end around the object and take a diagonal turn with it across the standing part (1).

Make a second identical turn, fitting it snugly between the first one and the standing part (2). Then finish off with a half hitch on the other side of the knot (3).

Work the knot snug and tight (4). The pull must be made on the side of the knot supported by the twin turns, so there is a 50:50 chance whether this version or its mirror-image is required.

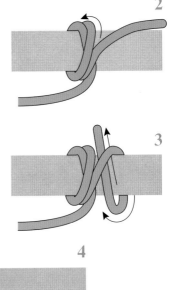

## ORIGIN

The name rolling hitch emerged around 1841. Older knotting manuals refer to it as the Magnus hitch or Magner's hitch, and today there is disagreement as to whether or not this was merely an earlier name for the same knot or if those names referred to the alternative way of tying it.

# ROUND TURN & TWO HALF HITCHES

Use this secure alternative to the clove hitch (*see pages 25 and 26*) when that knot is likely to prove inadequate. The round turn adds strength and supports the weight of the load; the two half hitches hold it in position.

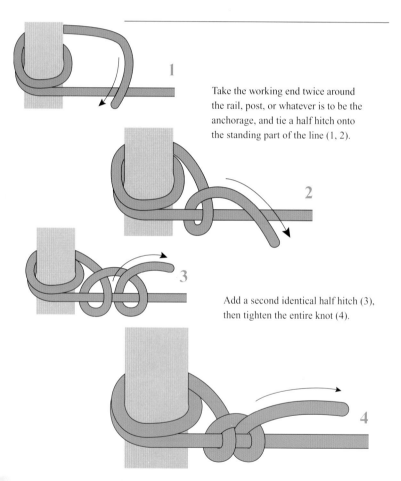

Take the working end twice around the rail, post, or whatever is to be the anchorage, and tie a half hitch onto the standing part of the line (1, 2).

Add a second identical half hitch (3), then tighten the entire knot (4).

## ORIGIN

This knot may be of enormous age and antiquity, although the name for it first appeared in *Elements & Practice of Rigging and Seamanship* (1794) by David Steel.

This knot is taught for its use with wet anchor warps, which can become slimed with seaweed, at which point the round turn & two half hitches (*see opposite*) could slip and even come undone. This modification should be employed whenever a more secure hitch is required.

Take a complete round turn with the working end, like a forward somersault, through the ring (1).

Then pass it behind the standing part and through the turn, to trap the initial half hitch (2).

Add a second identical half hitch and tighten the knot (3, 4).

# BOWLINE

The most common uses for a simple fixed loop like this one are either to start lashings and package ties or as a smartly applied and equally smartly cast-off hitch to a post.

Make an overhand loop (that is, one in which the line nearest to the working end lies on top) and tuck the end up through it, under, then over (1, 2).

**1**

Pass the end around behind the standing part and then tuck it down through the initial loop (3).

Tighten the knot, and secure the loose end by means of a double overhand knot around the nearest loop leg (4).

**2**

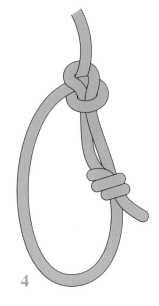

**3**

**4**

## ORIGIN

The name (pronounced "boh-linn") is a corruption of "bow line" and was used to refer to a rope that ran from the forward end of a ship to a square-sail yard, in certain sailing attitudes, so as to prevent it being accidentally taken aback (that is, blown inside out).

The common bowline (*see opposite*) can spill when tied in stiff or slippery line. This variation is just as strong but more secure, and will withstand being towed through water or dragged over rough ground.

**1**

Form an overhand loop (that is, one in which the working end lies on top of the standing part), then add a second identical one beneath it (1).

Tuck the working end up through each loop in turn, pass it around the standing part, then tuck it back down through both loops (2).

**2**

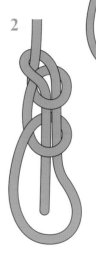

**3**

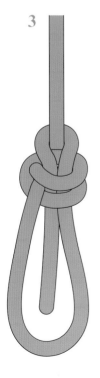

Tighten the knot in two stages, starting with the first loop. Then slide the second loop up to join its companion (3).

# DOUBLE ROUND TURN BOWLINE

The bowline, despite its pedigree, is not particularly strong or very secure. If these qualities are crucial to the knot's performance, use this tougher version instead, although being able to tie the common bowline (*see page 30*) will render this one easier.

Make an overhand loop, then add a second identical one on top of the first (1).

Tuck the working end up through both, before taking it around behind the standing part, and back down through both turns once more (2).

Tighten the knot (3).

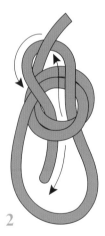

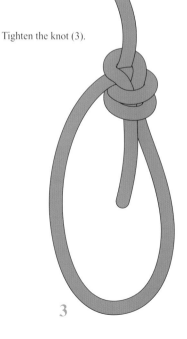

This is a quick and simple free-running noose to make.
It closes readily around whatever it contains, but cannot
jam and is therefore just as easily released.

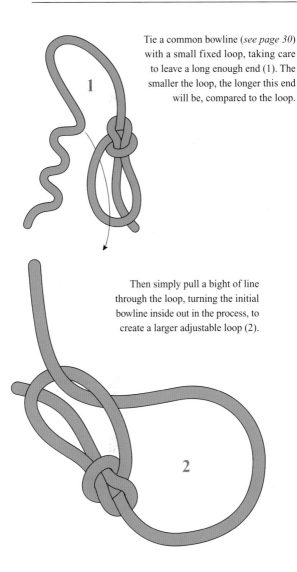

Tie a common bowline (*see page 30*)
with a small fixed loop, taking care
to leave a long enough end (1). The
smaller the loop, the longer this end
will be, compared to the loop.

Then simply pull a bight of line
through the loop, turning the initial
bowline inside out in the process, to
create a larger adjustable loop (2).

# REEF OR SQUARE KNOT

Use of this knot really must be limited to packages, first aid, and other small-scale items. It is a binding knot, usually tied in both ends of the same length of material, which relies for its security on being pressed against something (shoelace upon foot, bandage to limb, hair ribbon around braid, et cetera). But, as all knotting is a trade-off between convenience and reliability, plenty of occasions arise when this is all that is needed.

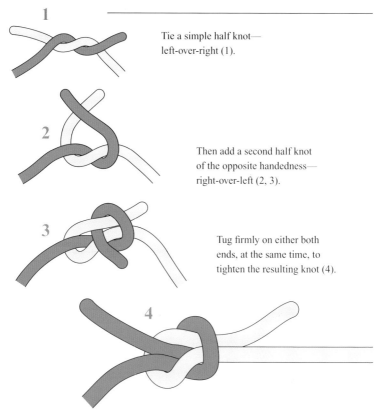

**1**

Tie a simple half knot— left-over-right (1).

**2**

Then add a second half knot of the opposite handedness— right-over-left (2, 3).

**3**

Tug firmly on either both ends, at the same time, to tighten the resulting knot (4).

**4**

## ORIGIN

The European name for this knot comes from its use on older sailboats for reefing sail, by folding or rolling lower sections of canvas and then securing them with a pair of cordage reefing points. The knot was known to the ancient Romans as the Hercules knot.

This layout has already been encountered in the common bowline (*see page 30*), but in this altered configuration joins two lines of slightly differing size or construction. A sheet bend should be tied so that both short ends occur on the same side, because the so-called "left-handed" version (with the ends on opposite sides) can in some cordage be less secure.

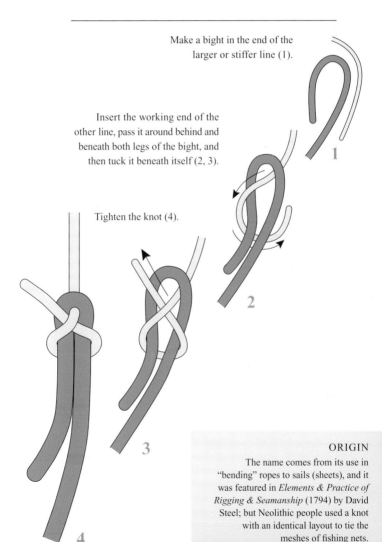

Make a bight in the end of the larger or stiffer line (1).

Insert the working end of the other line, pass it around behind and beneath both legs of the bight, and then tuck it beneath itself (2, 3).

Tighten the knot (4).

### ORIGIN

The name comes from its use in "bending" ropes to sails (sheets), and it was featured in *Elements & Practice of Rigging & Seamanship* (1794) by David Steel; but Neolithic people used a knot with an identical layout to tie the meshes of fishing nets.

# ONE-WAY SHEET BEND

The common sheet bend has the slight disadvantage that one end projects at right angles to the knot. If that could snag—for instance, when pulling the joined lines over or through a narrow gap—use this streamlined version instead.

**1**

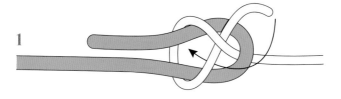

Tie a common sheet bend (*see page 35*) and then tuck the working end back beneath its own standing part (1).

**2**

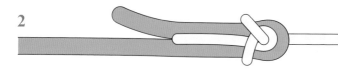

Tighten the knot so that three parts lie snugly together, all pointing in the same direction (2).

The common sheet bend (*see page 35*) can spill, if the lines that it joins are greatly dissimilar in either size or construction. If you are in any doubt, use the double sheet bend instead.

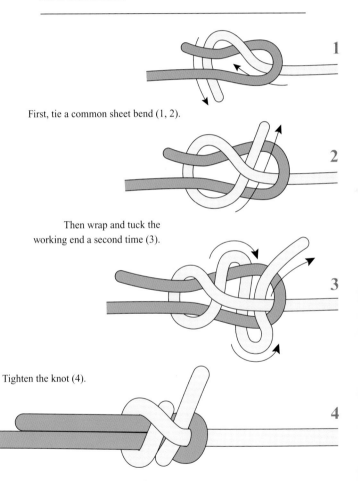

First, tie a common sheet bend (1, 2).

Then wrap and tuck the working end a second time (3).

Tighten the knot (4).

# FISHERMAN'S KNOT

Despite its misleading name, this knot—when tied in rope—is actually a bend. It is more secure than a sheet bend, but should be tied only in lines of the same size or construction.

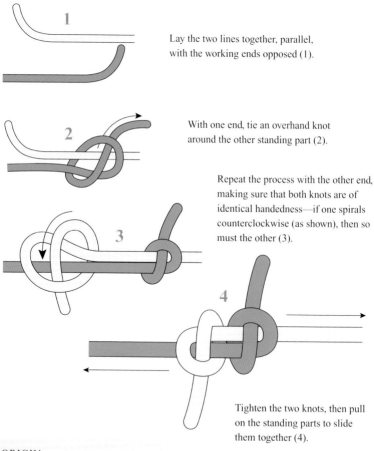

Lay the two lines together, parallel, with the working ends opposed (1).

With one end, tie an overhand knot around the other standing part (2).

Repeat the process with the other end, making sure that both knots are of identical handedness—if one spirals counterclockwise (as shown), then so must the other (3).

Tighten the two knots, then pull on the standing parts to slide them together (4).

## ORIGIN

As the convention is that bends and hitches tied in small stuff are simply called "knots," the name of this knot presumably originated with medieval anglers and was tied in fishing lines of horsehair or gut.

# DOUBLE FISHERMAN'S KNOT

More wrapping turns imbue a knot with greater strength and make it more secure, which is why this bulked-up version of the fisherman's knot (*see opposite*) is popular with climbers and cavers, who use it to create endless slings or strops. It is not easily undone, however, once it has been heavily loaded.

Lay the two lines alongside one another, parallel, with the ends opposed (1).

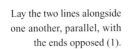

With one end, tie a double overhand knot around the other standing part (2).

Repeat the process with the other end, ensuring that both knots have the same handedness—if one spirals counterclockwise (as shown), then so must the other (3).

Tighten both knots, then pull on the standing ends to slide them together (4).

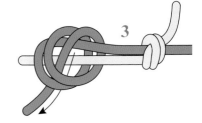

### ORIGIN
The basic fisherman's knot is unsuitable for most modern nylon fishing lines, but the doubled version is employed by anglers, who know it as the grinner knot, presumably because of the smiley mouth made with the two lines between the knots while they remain apart.

# TRIPLE FISHERMAN'S KNOT

For still greater strength and security, anglers and climbers in particular favor this muscle-bound version of the basic knot, which anglers call a double grinner knot.

Lay the two lines alongside one another, parallel, with the ends opposed. With one working end, tie a triple overhand knot around the other standing part (1, 2).

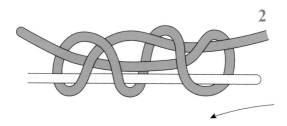

Repeat the process with the other end, ensuring that both knots have the same handedness—if one spirals counterclockwise (as shown), then so must the other. Tighten both knots, then pull on the standing ends to slide them together (3).

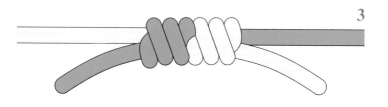

# 20 PRACTICAL KNOTS

*"Just about all knots are useful . . ."*

<small>CHARLES WARNER, 1992</small>

Knots make rope work and, while it is possible to use (and sometimes to misuse or abuse) the same old ones for every task that comes along, having a wider repertoire literally at one's fingertips is a better strategy.

# INTRODUCTION

Learning to tie any knot is easier when you know what the completed knot looks like, so this book includes both step-by-step tying stages and an image of the tied and tightened knot. There is, however, more than one way to tie most knots, and in *The Directory of Knots* the one that is depicted is generally just the method considered easiest to learn, or in some cases the one that could be most clearly illustrated. Learn it—you will certainly not be wasting your time.

Here is a tip that can lead to discovering another quicker and more fluent tying method for some knots. Some hitches, when removed from their rail, post, or other anchoring foundation, fall apart until nothing of them remains. Examples in this section are the pole hitch and the cat's paw. And some loops, if a retaining bight is withdrawn from them, also collapse and vanish. The angler's loop is a prime example. Knots like this, which can (to put it pedantically) be "untied in the bight" can also be tied "in the bight"—that is, without using either end of the line. Applying this test can reveal a distinct difference between knots that otherwise are only a tuck or turn apart in their makeup. For instance, the constrictor knot can be tied in the bight, but the strangle knot cannot; and untying in the bight often instructs you in how to tie the knot in the bight.

This previously unsuspected relationship was identified and defined as the Law of Loop, Hitch & Bight by Dr. Harry Asher, M.A., Ph.D., who first published it in *A New System of Knotting* (1986) and later in his *Alternative Knot Book* (1989). Tying a knot in the bight can be a quick and efficient (almost sleight-of-hand) method, with the obvious advantage that it can be done even when neither end of the line is accessible. It is always worth learning to do.

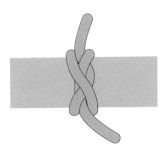

*Constrictor knot tied in the bight*

# STEVEDORE KNOT

Dock workers whose livelihood involved hoisting and moving loads by means of simple block-&-tackle used this knot in preference to the basic figure-eight stopper (*see page 22*). It does not block a bigger hole, but is bulkier and easier to untie when the rope must be continually removed from one pulley to another.

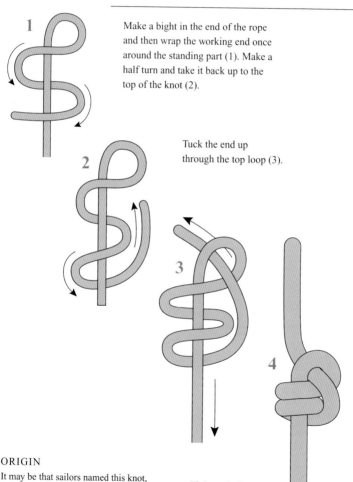

Make a bight in the end of the rope and then wrap the working end once around the standing part (1). Make a half turn and take it back up to the top of the knot (2).

Tuck the end up through the top loop (3).

Tighten the knot (4).

## ORIGIN

It may be that sailors named this knot, having seen it tied by longshoremen or stevedores on the quayside.

# ASHLEY'S STOPPER KNOT

When the figure-eight and stevedore stopper knots prove inadequate, enabling the rope in which they are tied to pull free, then use this chunky alternative. Originally called the oysterman's stopper knot, it has now become a favorite with knot tyers and a minor classic.

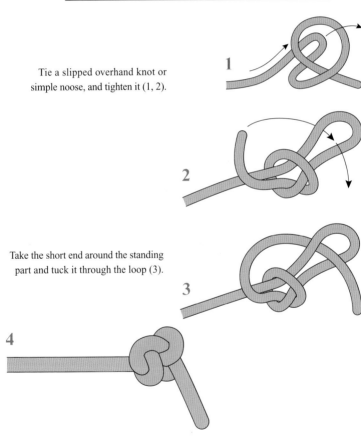

Tie a slipped overhand knot or simple noose, and tighten it (1, 2).

Take the short end around the standing part and tuck it through the loop (3).

Pull down on the standing part to shrink the loop and trap the end (4).

## ORIGIN

This knot was devised by American book illustrator and author Clifford Warren Ashley more than 90 years ago. Having spotted a knot he could not identify aboard an oyster-fishing boat, this was his attempt to reproduce it, although he later found it to be merely a figure-eight knot.

# STRANGLE KNOT

This alternative to the constrictor knot (*see opposite*) is preferred by some knot tyers because the turns bed-down more snugly; but, unlike the constrictor, it cannot be tied in the bight. The strangle knot is actually a double overhand knot tied loosely, then slipped over and around something (rope's end, sack neck, roll of wallpaper) as a ligature, instead of as a mere stopper knot.

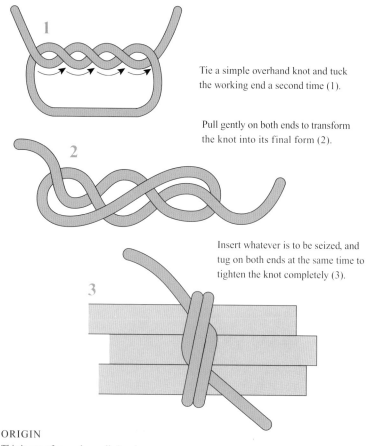

Tie a simple overhand knot and tuck the working end a second time (1).

Pull gently on both ends to transform the knot into its final form (2).

Insert whatever is to be seized, and tug on both ends at the same time to tighten the knot completely (3).

## ORIGIN

This is one of several so-called sack or miller's knots that were once required to tie off the flax, jute, or hessian bags that our ancestors used to hold bushels or pecks of grain, seed, flour, and other staple commodities produced by windmills and the later factories.

# CONSTRICTOR KNOT
# TIED WITH AN END

This is probably the world's best seizing knot, so secure that it has to be cut off after use. It makes a rapid first-aid tourniquet for the cut end of a rope, to prevent it fraying and unraveling, which can be left in place to become a semipermanent binding. It will also hold a hose on a faucet, clamp woodwork while glue dries, or attach pencil to string for use on a clipboard.

Pass the working end of a length of cord or twine around the item to be bound, then cross it diagonally over the initial turn (1).

Take the end once more around the foundation, and then tuck it over (the standing part), under, under, as shown (2, 3).

Pull strongly on both ends to tighten this knot, using pliers or other aids for the tightest possible grip (4).

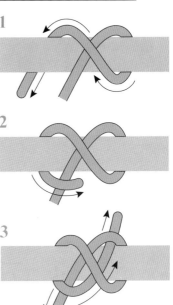

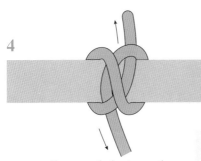

To remove the knot, sever the overriding diagonal knot part. The knot will fall away in two cut segments, without damage to whatever lay beneath it.

## ORIGIN

This knot is believed to be one of 18 described (but not illustrated) in a brief essay on surgical slings by the Greek physician Heraklas, in the first century AD. It may also have been the so-called gunner's knot, and was used as a whip knot by Spanish muleteers in the 1930s.

# CONSTRICTOR KNOT WITH DRAWLOOP

Although the constrictor is essentially a semipermanent seizing, it can also be resorted to as the most temporary of holdfasts, in which case it makes sense to tie it without pulling the working end completely through the knot. The result is a drawloop that can later be used to release the knot—no knife needed.

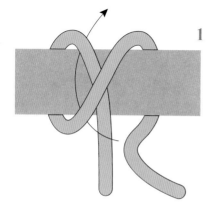

Wrap and cross the working end, as shown (1).

Then simply pull a bight from the working end, bring it in front of the standing part, and tuck—under, under—to complete the knot (2). Tighten.

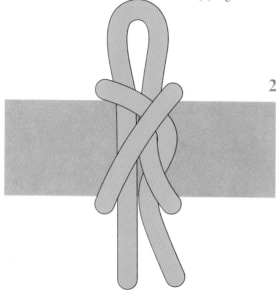

# CONSTRICTOR KNOT
# TIED IN THE BIGHT

When it can be done, tying any knot "in the bight" (that is to say, without using either end of the line) is invariably quicker. Indeed, the dexterity engendered is almost sleight of hand. So, when the end of the rope, hose, or other item to be seized is accessible, tie the basic constrictor knot this way.

Take a turn with the working end and pull out a bight from the lower part (1).

Bring it around and across the other knot parts to pass over the end of the foundation (2, 3).

Tighten the knot in the usual manner (4).

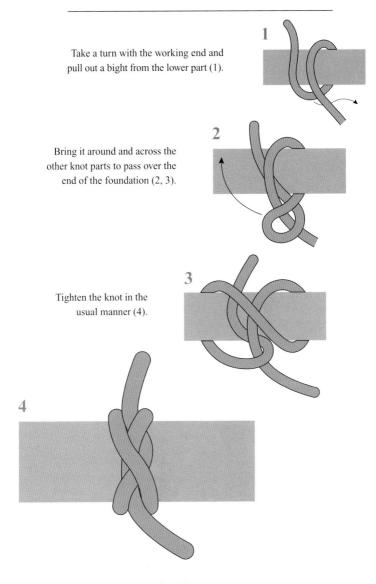

# Double constrictor knot tied with an end

You can employ this reinforced version of the basic constrictor knot in any situation where the reliability of the latter may be doubtful.

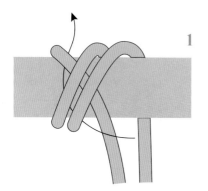

**1**

Take a turn around the foundation and lead the working end diagonally across its standing part, as if tying the basic knot, then add a second diagonal alongside the first one (1).

Tuck the working end—over one, under two, under one—as shown, and then tighten the resulting knot (2).

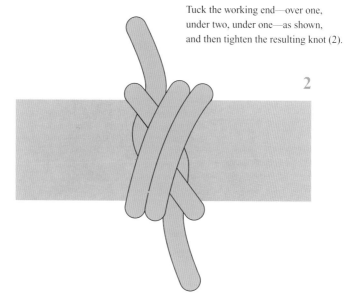

**2**

# DOUBLE CONSTRICTOR
# KNOT TIED IN THE BIGHT

Tying in the bight is always preferable and, provided
the end of the item to be seized is accessible, the double
constrictor knot can be achieved this way.

First, tie a clove hitch (*see page
25*), then pull out a bight from
behind the upper loose end (1, 2).

Wrap the bight down and
around, passing over the end of the
foundation, to create a second
diagonal alongside the first one (3).

Tighten the knot (4).

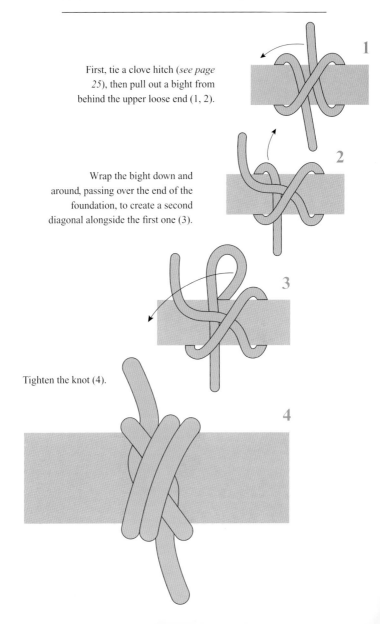

# POLE HITCH

For making and carrying bundles (ranging from garden trellis sticks to sailboat masts and spars), a pair of these knots is unbeatable.

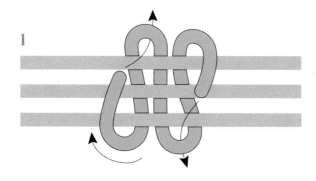

Lay out the lashing in an S or Z shape and place the items to be lashed together on top (1).

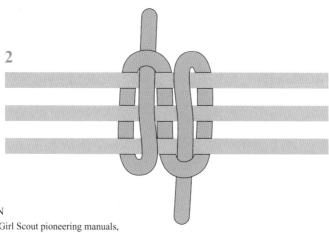

## ORIGIN

Boy and Girl Scout pioneering manuals, more than any other, have preserved the knowledge of this knot.

Tuck each end of the line through the opposite bight (2).

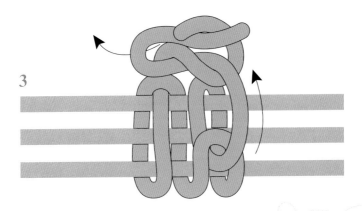

3

Then pull up on both ends to wrap
the twin bights firmly around the
load they now contain (3).

Lastly, tie off the two ends with a reef
or square knot (4). Add a second pole
hitch at the other end of long items.

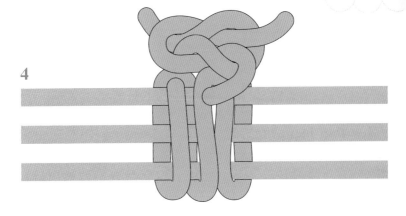

4

# BUNTLINE HITCH

When a line is attached to a ring or other item of hardware that is likely to be continually shaken or otherwise disturbed (for example, when tied to a sail or flag halyard), use this secure, yet compact knot. Because the short end is trapped against the anchorage point, it is unlikely to come loose, although that can also make it awkward to untie. It is dual-purpose, however, working equally well in cordage or flat webbing.

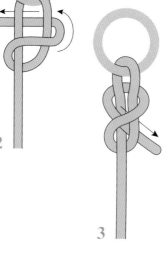

Pass the working end through the ring or other point of attachment, then wrap and tuck it, as shown (1, 2, 3). The result is a clove hitch (*see page 25*) tied around the standing part of the line.

Tighten the knot itself, and then slide it up snug against the ring (4).

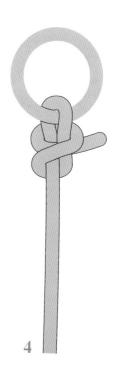

**1**

**2**

**3**

**4**

## ORIGIN

Buntlines were ropes that hung loose from a ship's topsails, where they were subjected to severe wind disturbance, and so only a secure knot would do to attach them. When the necktie superseded the cravat as an item of wear, this was the knot taught by generations of fathers to sons.

# OSSEL HITCH

This resilient little hitch was frequently used by sea fisherman to suspend their driftnets from short vertical lengths of cord. It had to cope with being tugged about by underwater movement and proved a reliable, yet simple knot for the job.

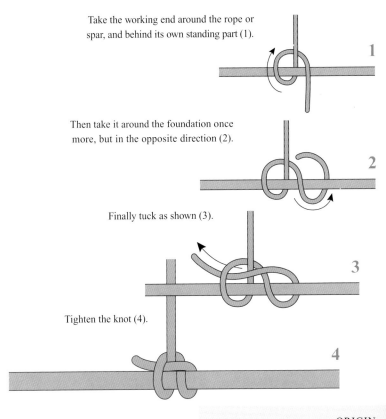

Take the working end around the rope or spar, and behind its own standing part (1).

**1**

Then take it around the foundation once more, but in the opposite direction (2).

**2**

Finally tuck as shown (3).

**3**

Tighten the knot (4).

**4**

## ORIGIN

The word "ossel" (or sometimes "orsel") is a British regional version of "norsel" (for the length of cord that connects gill nets to their head-ropes).

# OSSEL KNOT

The ossel knot is a kissing cousin of the ossel hitch (*see page 55*), but is employed as a fishing knot closer to the surface of the sea than its relative. There conditions are rougher and so it must be more robust.

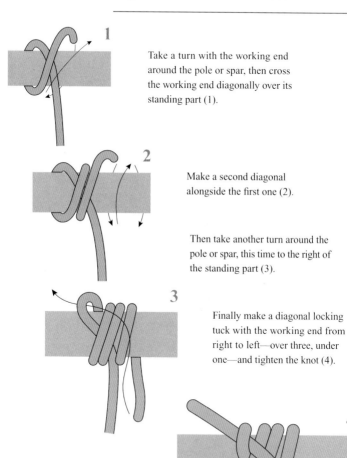

Take a turn with the working end around the pole or spar, then cross the working end diagonally over its standing part (1).

Make a second diagonal alongside the first one (2).

Then take another turn around the pole or spar, this time to the right of the standing part (3).

Finally make a diagonal locking tuck with the working end from right to left—over three, under one—and tighten the knot (4).

# CAT'S PAW

This is a tried-and-trusted old hook or ring hitch that has been tied in rope (by dockers) and in nylon monofilaments (by anglers).

Take a long loop, or make a bight in the end of the line, and bend it down to create twin loops (1).

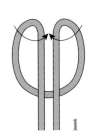

Twist one loop clockwise, the other counterclockwise, imparting the same number of turns to each (2, 3).

Place the line over the hook, or other point of attachment, and tighten the knot by pulling down on both legs (4).

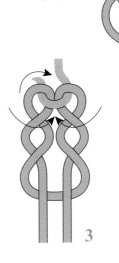

### ORIGIN
The name is derived from the fanciful likeness to a cat's paw, but today anglers generally know this knot as the offshore swivel knot.

# TIMBER HITCH

This almost knotless knot will drag or tow lumber, piling, scaffold poles, or any other imaginable load over rough terrain or through water. London's river police, before they were equipped with more sanitary methods of retrieval, used it to haul drowned corpses from the Thames.

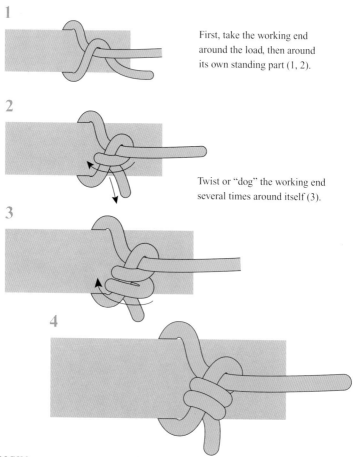

**1**

First, take the working end around the load, then around its own standing part (1, 2).

**2**

Twist or "dog" the working end several times around itself (3).

**3**

**4**

## ORIGIN

The term timber hitch was mentioned in *A Treatise of Rigging* (ca. 1625), but was not illustrated until it appeared later in *L'Encyclopédie* (1762) by Denis Diderot.

Slide the resulting noose tight (4).

# Killick hitch

When long objects are dragged or towed by a timber hitch, they tend to sheer off course unless they are given some directional stability. The killick hitch performs just this function.

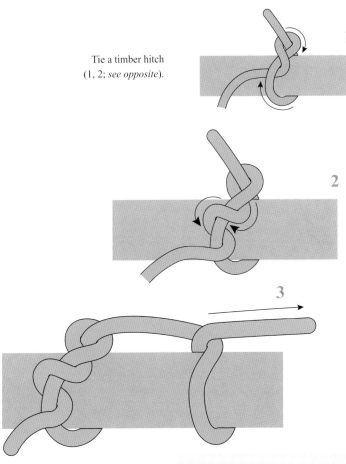

Tie a timber hitch
(1, 2; *see opposite*).

**1**

**2**

**3**

Now add one or more half hitches, in the direction from which the pull will be applied (3).

### ORIGIN

A "killick" was a small improvised anchor, which would be attached to the rope anchor warp, or to the buoy line marking lobster pots on the seabed, by means of this knot, which was named and illustrated in David Steel's *Elements & Practice of Rigging & Seamanship* (1794).

# WATER KNOT

Tied in cordage, this knot is hard to untie after it has been loaded. So its use is best restricted to package string and other trivial jobs. In flat tape or webbing, however, it is a highly regarded and recommended knot for climbing slings and harnesses (when it is known as a tape knot).

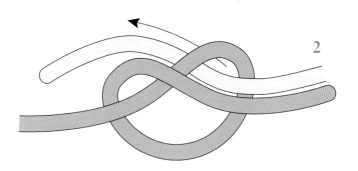

In one end of one line, tie an overhand knot (1).

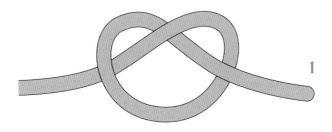

Insert the working end of the other line, and follow the original lead around to reproduce the knot, in the process doubling its ply (2, 3).

## ORIGIN

This seems to be another angling knot from the English Middle Ages. Indeed, it may be the "water knot" mentioned by the legendary Prioress of Sopwell, Dame Juliana, in the *Treatyse of Fyshinge wyth an Angle* (1496), although it is uncertain whether or not she really wrote that book.

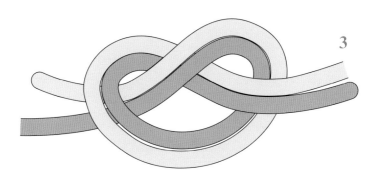

**3**

Rearrange the initial layout, if necessary, so that the load falling upon the standing parts is exerted at the outside ends of the knot (4)—it is stronger that way. If the standing parts cross directly at the heart of the knot, then in time they could chafe or saw through one another.

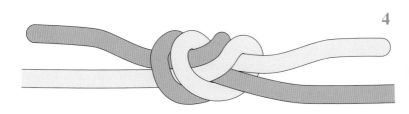

**4**

# FIGURE-EIGHT BEND

This is a fairly strong bend that, depending on the stuff in which it is tied, is generally easier to untie than the water knot (*see pages 60–61*). Unlike that versatile knot, it is unsuitable for tape or webbing.

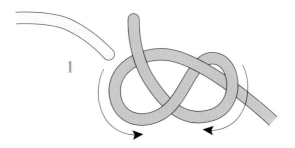

In one end of one line, tie a figure-eight knot (1).

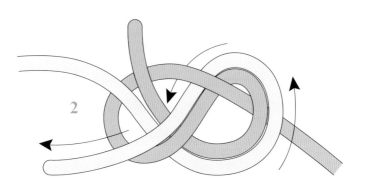

Insert the working end of the other line, and follow the initial lead around to reproduce the knot (2, 3).

## ORIGIN

Just as the figure-eight stopper knot (*see page 22*) was once known as the Flemish knot, so this was called the Flemish bend.

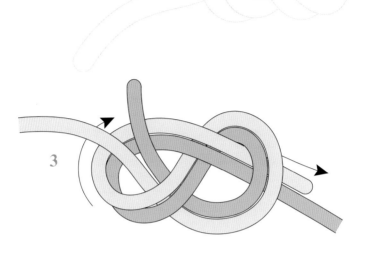

3

Then tighten the knot (4).

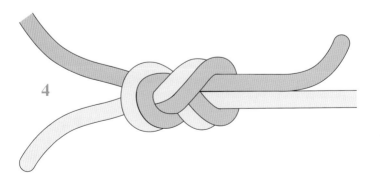

4

# CARRICK BEND

This bend is intended for use in large hawsers or cables that do not accept very tight bends and tucks. Use it instead of the fisherman's knot and the sheet bend.

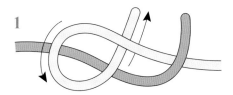

Form an underhand loop (one in which the line nearest the working end goes beneath the standing part), then lay the end of the other line beneath the loop and over the standing part, as shown (1).

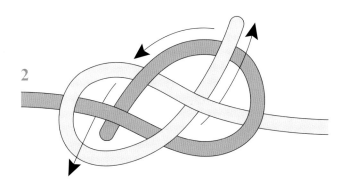

Continuing counterclockwise, make a locking tuck going over, under, over (2).

### ORIGIN

The word "carrick" is something of a puzzle in knot-tying circles. A "carrack" was a type of medieval merchant ship; and there is a Carrick Roads in Falmouth harbour, Cornwall. The knot name appears in the *Vocabulaire des Termes de Marine* (1783) by M. Lescallier.

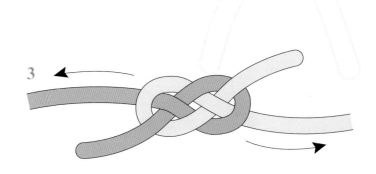

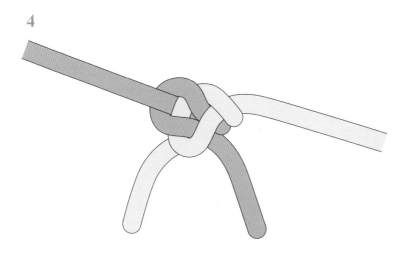

Then begin to tighten the knot (3).

Let the knot capsize into its final form (4), which is unrecognizable from the initial layout.

However, the knot is found as a decorative motif in the much earlier Elizabethan plasterwork of Ormonde Castle at Carrick-on-Suir, Ireland. Earlier still, it was the badge of the rebel English leader Hereward the Wake, who opposed William the Conqueror in 1070; and it is still occasionally called the Wake knot.

# ZEPPELIN BEND

There is an entire family of bends made up from a couple of interlocked overhand knots, of which this is the easiest to tie right every time. It is also a proven workhorse (*see Origin below*).

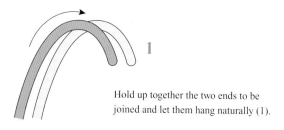

Hold up together the two ends to be joined and let them hang naturally (1).

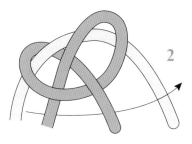

Tie an overhand knot in the foremost one, enclosing the standing part of the other (2).

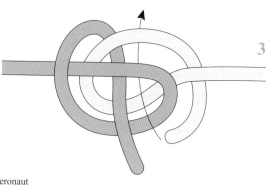

## ORIGIN

The heroic American aeronaut Lieutenant-Commander Charles Rosendahl is said to have insisted that the bow line of the airship he commanded in the 1930s (the zeppelin *Los Angeles*) was attached to her ground mooring lines with this knot.

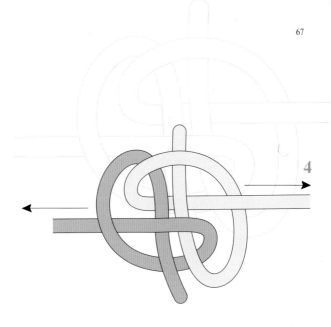

**4**

Then bring that standing part forward and tuck its working end up through the central compartments made by both strands (3, 4).

Tighten the knot (5).

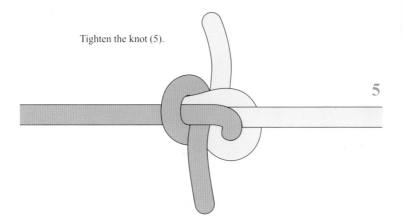

**5**

The knot remained in use by the U.S. Navy until 1962 for securing lighter-than-air craft—those instructors who knew its history referred to it as the Rosendahl bend. Two journalists, Bob and Lee Payne, assigned it the Z-word in an article for *Boating* magazine in 1976.

# ANGLER'S LOOP

This all-purpose fixed loop works perfectly (its other name is the perfection loop) in rope, cord, twine, and some fishing lines. It even captures and holds bungee cord, which wriggles free from many otherwise dependable knots.

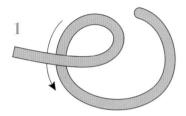

Form an underhand loop (one in which the part of the line nearest the working end goes underneath the standing part) (1).

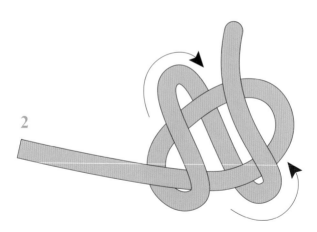

Then wrap the end completely around both legs of the loop, as shown (2).

### ORIGIN

This is an age-old angling knot, a survivor from the days of horsehair and gut fishing lines. At one time it was viewed with disfavor by rope workers because it would jam in vegetable-fiber cordage. In today's synthetic ropes and cords, however, it is ideal.

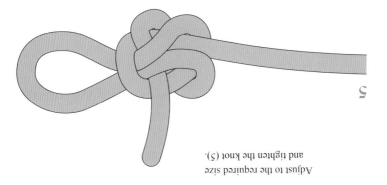

Adjust to the required size
and tighten the knot (5).

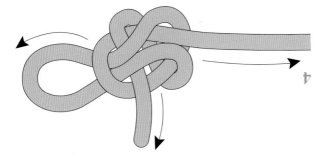

Pull a bight from the first of the
turns over the second one and
down through the initial loop (3, 4).

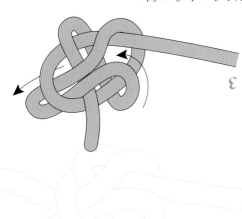

# MIDSHIPMAN'S LOOP

This is one of those slide-&-grip loop knots, useful when tent guylines, laundry lines, and such like must be slackened off or tightened to cope with varying conditions. In the artisan's workshop and the artist's studio it has also proved its worth for suspending bits and pieces, when two hands prove insufficient.

Pass the end around, through, or over the rail, ring, post, or other anchorage point and make an overhand loop (one in which that part of the line nearest the working end goes over the standing part) (1).

Tuck the end through the loop, lay it diagonally over itself, then insert a second similar diagonal snugly between the first one and the upper loop leg (2, 3).

## ORIGIN

The name implies use aboard naval warships during the days of sail, when a midshipman was a more senior or experienced rank than the junior one it became in modern times.

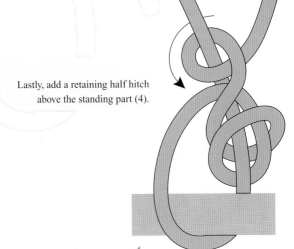

Lastly, add a retaining half hitch above the standing part (4).

**4**

Tighten the knot, carefully eliminating all of the slack, so that what results is in effect a rolling hitch (*see page 27*) that slides (5). The knot may be shifted readily enough by hand to alter the size of the loop; but, when loaded, it will hold firm.

**5**

# BOWLINE IN THE BIGHT

Twin fixed loops can be used to spread a load or share it between two separate anchorage points. This variation of the common bowline (*see page 30*) has the advantage that it can be tied in the bight.

**1**

Take a loop, or make a bight, and cast an overhand loop (one in which the twin parts of the line closest to the end of the original loop or bight go over the standing parts) (1).

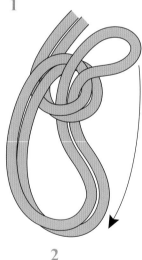

**2**

Tuck the end of the loop or bight up through this loop, from back to front (2).

## ORIGIN

Like many other twin-loop knots, the bowline in the bight almost certainly came into existence as an improvised chair knot in which a workman sat suspended—one loop beneath his thighs, the other around his chest and armpits— to work up masts, down wells, etc.

Assuming that the standing parts of the line are too long to tuck through in the usual way, bend the bight down in front of the uncompleted knot and pass the two large loops through it (3).

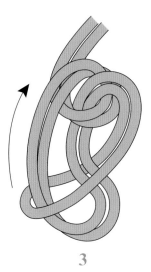

**3**

Then lift the bight up once more behind the standing parts (4). This knot almost tightens itself, but should be made snug by hand before use. See how the entire knot is doubled, except for the retaining bight around the standing parts, which remains single.

**4**

In these more safety-conscious and litigious times, such use is not recommended; approved safety harnesses should be preferred. Nevertheless, in an emergency when nothing else is available, a knowledge of such knots may still prove invaluable.

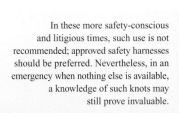

# TOM FOOL'S KNOT

The name of this knot implies—wrongly—that it is somehow weak, impractical, and not to be used. In fact, a study in 1996 by British professional firefighter Colin Grundy, of rope-chair rescue knots, determined that it was equal in effectiveness to the generally preferred handcuff knot on the opposite page.

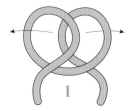

Form an alternating pair of loops, one overhand, the other underhand, and overlap them as shown (1).

Then simply pull a bight from the right-hand loop through the left-hand loop, and vice versa (2).

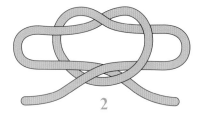

Pull on the lower loop legs to adjust them to the required size, then pull on the upper loop legs to tighten the knot (3).

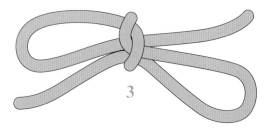

## ORIGIN

In the various British fire brigades, this knot has been the basis for an emergency human-rescue knot since the chair knot (as firemen refer to it), or fireman's chair knot (as it is known to everyone else), was introduced by the Victorian chief officer, Eyre Massey-Shaw, in 1876.

# HANDCUFF KNOT

Unlike the bowline in the bight (*see pages 72–73*),
this knot (which is liked by young knot tyers because it
challenges their abilities as would-be escape artists) has
adjustable loops.

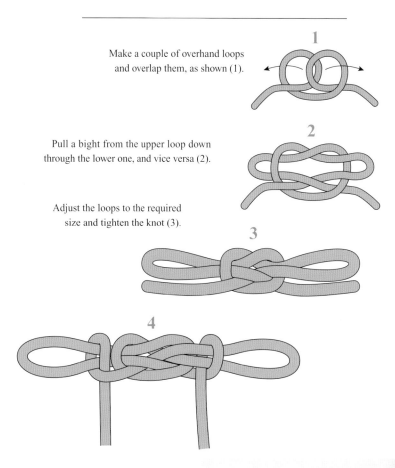

Make a couple of overhand loops
and overlap them, as shown (1).

Pull a bight from the upper loop down
through the lower one, and vice versa (2).

Adjust the loops to the required
size and tighten the knot (3).

To lock each loop in position, tie
a half hitch around it with the
adjacent standing part (4).

### ORIGIN

It is most likely that so-called handcuff
knots actually evolved to hobble animals,
leting them graze over a limited area, but
preventing them straying too far from
overnight campsites. They also have a
history as emergency chair knots, used in
particular by fire rescue services.

# LAPP KNOT

Knots that incorporate a drawloop as a quick-release can often leave fingers and fingernails with a final bit of untying. The Lapp knot is pure escapism: tug the short end and it falls apart. Unjustly dismissed by some as a "false" sheet bend, this knot has in fact been known for at least a century.

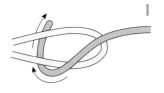

**1**

Tie a loop or make a bight in one of the ends to be joined and lay the end of the other line on top of it (1).

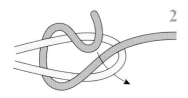

**2**

Wrap the working end around both legs of the loop or bight and make a retaining tuck with a bight from the working end, over its own standing part and down through the initial loop or bight (2, 3).

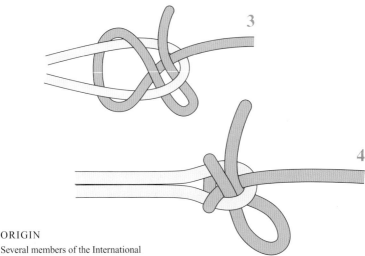

**3**

**4**

### ORIGIN

Several members of the International Guild of Knot Tyers confirm this knot's distinct and discrete identity. In the Guild's April 1996 issue of *Knotting Matters,* Robert Pont of France reported having seen it used in Lapland to secure knife lanyards and hitch reindeer to sleds.

Carefully tighten the knot into a stable and secure, compact form (4).

# TRADITIONAL KNOTS

*"Old knots never die; they just wait for us to come to our senses."*

BRION TOSS, 1992

There is a generous legacy of knots bequeathed to us by our ancestors, who employed them in multifarious ways. Wilderness pioneers lashed loads to pack animals, bucketed water from wells, and probed the earth for ores and oil. The first large buildings were erected using rope tackles and lashed scaffolding, and on a smaller scale individual farmers and storekeepers, shoe menders, bookbinders, and weavers all relied upon a much-used knot or two. A selection of these time-honored (and never outmoded) knots follows.

# INTRODUCTION

Whether a knot is tied "in the bight" (that is, without using either end of the line) or not, the working end can often either be pulled completely through the finished knot or left protruding in the form of a small bight, known as a drawloop. Knots with drawloops are termed "slipped-knots."

A drawloop does not, it must be stressed, convert any knot into a life-saving, quick-release hitch (such as the Lapp knot on page 76). It merely ensures that the knot incorporating it can be undone without breaking fingernails in the process. Nevertheless, drawloops ought to be used more than they currently are, since they do not weaken the knots in which they appear. In fact, they may actually strengthen them by the inclusion of an extra section of rope or cord. Security will not be increased and may, depending upon what knot and what material are used, actually be reduced somewhat; but, as knots are more often than not tight enough for what they are required to do, that may be no bad thing. Examples of traditional knots with drawloops in this section are the ground line hitch and the horse dealer's hitch.

The drawloop is just one instance of a phenomenon that a periodic contributor to *Knotting Matters*, writing under the pen-name Cy Canute, described in September 2000 as the "parsimonious"—in other words, economical, mean, or stingy—nature of knotting.

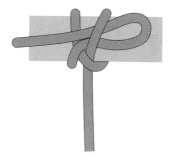

*Ground line hitch with drawloop*

Other instances of this parsimony principle are: that bowlines and sheet bends have similar layouts, so learn one and the other comes virtually free in terms of time and effort; adjustable nooses are commonly locked by the addition of half hitches; many traditional knots have as their basis the overhand and figure-eight knots; and bulky knots with lots of wrapping turns (collectively referred to as "blood knots") can usually be reckoned very strong knots. Be alert for such shared features and a large repertoire of interrelated knots will be more easily acquired.

# GOOD-LUCK OR SHAMROCK LANYARD KNOT

A lanyard is a short length of cord, attached to a belt or hung around the neck, to retain anything from a knife or stopwatch to a lucky charm. Lanyard knots serve either to form a retaining loop for whatever is to be attached to the cord, to embellish it, or (as in this case) to do both at once.

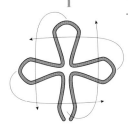

Double the length of cord and pull out three fingerlike bights (1).

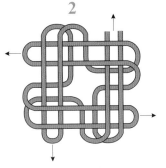

Pick up the two standing parts and lay them to the right, over the adjacent bight. Place this bight over the next bight, continuing counterclockwise. Then put the second bight across the third, and make a locking tuck with the third beneath the twin loops created by the initial move (2).

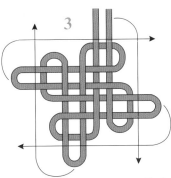

## ORIGIN

This knot is one of the simplest in an ancient Oriental series of increasingly elaborate crown knots, but was named only as recently as 1981 by knotting writer Lydia Chen in her book *Chinese Knotting*.

Gradually work this crown knot, as it is called, snug. Pull each knot part in turn to eliminate all the unwanted slack. Take care that pairs of strands lie parallel—like rail tracks—and do not twist or cross each other. Then, *without turning the work over*, start making a clockwise crown knot (3).

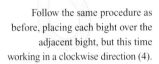

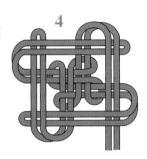

**4**

Follow the same procedure as before, placing each bight over the adjacent bight, but this time working in a clockwise direction (4).

Tighten this second stage, adjusting the three primary loops to the required size, and (as optional ornamentation) create four smaller secondary loops in the final knot (5).

**5**

If you start with four bights instead of three, then a five-part shamrock knot may also be tied (6).

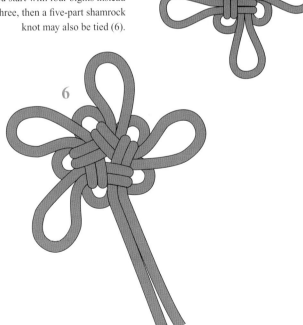

**6**

# CHINESE LANYARD KNOT

This ornamental knot is simpler to tie than it appears on the printed page, although tightening to achieve the unusual square outline requires care and patience. But nothing ventured, nothing gained.

Double a length of cord and, leaving a bight, tie a pair of matching half knots. After a gap, tie a similar pair of half knots (1).

Bring the bight up, inverting the lower pair of half knots in the process; and, having also inverted the upper pair of half knots, tuck the bight up through the center of them (2).

Similarly, tuck both loose ends down through the center of the lower pair of half knots, exactly as shown (3). The tying is now completed.

**1**

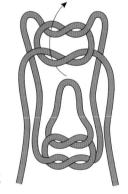

**2**

**3**

## ORIGIN

Lydia Chen, in her book *Chinese Knotting* (1981), calls this by its alternative name of plafond knot, after the highly decorated ceilings (or *plafonds*) of Chinese temples, where the knot pattern appears repeatedly as an ornamental motif.

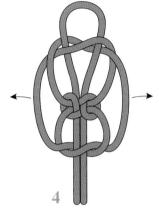

First, tighten the four-part crown that is the centerpiece of this knot, then close up the remaining upper and lower half knots (4).

**4**

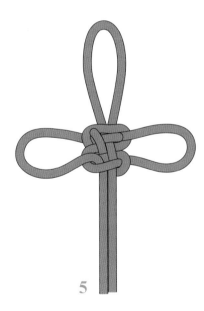

**5**

**6**

Lastly, eliminate each side loop by painstakingly working the unwanted slack through the knot until it emerges at one or other of the loose ends, taking care to impart equal tension to every knot part (5, 6).

# MOORING HITCH

This alternative to the clove hitch (*see pages 25 and 26*) is quickly tied in the bight and slipped over a vertical mooring post. It may be used to secure a dinghy or even a compliant animal, provided that both are kept under observation.

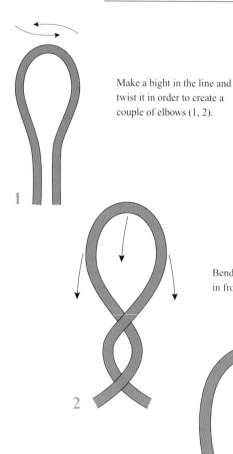

Make a bight in the line and twist it in order to create a couple of elbows (1, 2).

Bend the upper loop down in front, as shown (3).

## ORIGIN

This tying method was proposed and published as recently as December 2001 by knot craftsman Brian Jarrett of the English county of Kent, although the hitch itself is much older.

Then simply slide the resulting layout over the mooring post, as illustrated (4, 5) and tighten the knot.

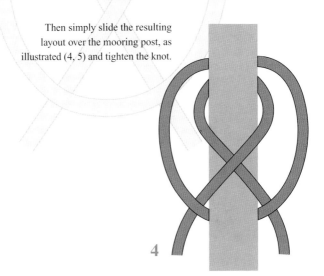

4

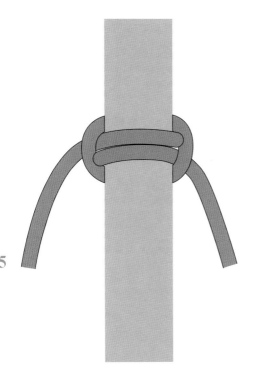

5

# TURK'S HEAD
## 3L x 4B

A Turk's head is a braided bracelet of a knot. The number of different Turk's heads is virtually infinite, but this basic specimen, with its three interwoven parts (leads, L) and four overlapping rim parts (bights, B), is a popular specimen with a variety of uses. It can seize or whip the cut end of a rope to prevent it fraying, or embellish items as diverse as table lamps and flower pots. Tied in gold or silver wire, it makes an unusual finger ring; it is also the sliding neckerchief ring known to young Scouts as a "woggle."

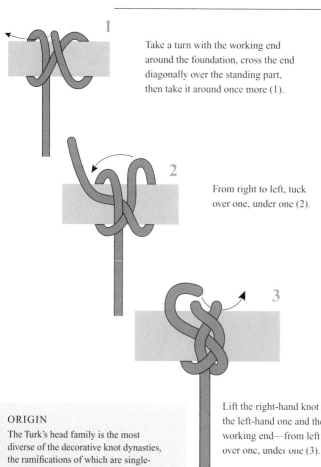

**1**

Take a turn with the working end around the foundation, cross the end diagonally over the standing part, then take it around once more (1).

**2**

From right to left, tuck over one, under one (2).

**3**

Lift the right-hand knot part across the left-hand one and then tuck the working end—from left to right—over one, under one (3).

## ORIGIN

The Turk's head family is the most diverse of the decorative knot dynasties, the ramifications of which are single-mindedly pursued by some knot tyers, and entire publications have been written about it. Like most knot lore, the tale of its origin is apocryphal.

**4**

Bring the working end around
and tuck it beside its own
standing part (4, 5).

**5**

Follow the original lead around,
going over where it goes over, under
where it goes under, to double and
triple the ply of the knot (6).

**6**

It is said that the Turk's head got its
name because the basic knot resembles a
turban, and the sailormen of yore called
anyone east of Suez who wore this form
of headgear (whether Muslim, Hindu,
or Sikh) "a Turk." However, the knot is
probably Spanish, and was spread by
means of trade and conquest.

# TURK'S HEAD
## 4L x 3B

Every Turk's head knot is identified by two dimensions: first, the number of braided "leads" (pronounced "leeds") that determine its width; second, by the number of rim parts, or bights, that make up its circumference. Use this four-lead by three-bight (4L x 3B) Turk's head knot when the 3L x 4B version (*see pages 86–87*) is too narrow for the purpose in hand.

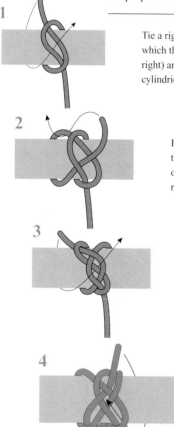

Tie a right-handed half knot (one in which the two knot parts spiral to the right) around the rope, rod, or other cylindrical foundation (1).

Bring the working end around and tuck up—from left to right—under one, over one. Then tuck down—from right to left—over one, under one (2).

Bring the working end around to the front once more and make a locking tuck up—from left to right—over one, under one, over one (3).

Finally bring the working end down and around to be inserted, under, over, alongside its own standing part (4). By following the original lead with the working end, the knot can be converted into two- or three-ply (5).

# Turk's head
## 3L x 5B

Some members of the Turk's head family not only serve as bracelets, but also look good when tied flat. This one makes a neat table mat or coaster, an appliqué picture in a frame, and—in rope—can serve as a tough clump mat to protect the woodwork or fiberglass of a smart sailboat from dents and scars caused by blocks and other items of rigging hardware.

Make the outline of a pretzel (but unknotted), then tuck the working end as shown, going over one, under one, over one (1).

**1**

Continuing clockwise, make a locking tuck under one, over one, under one, over one (2).

**2**

Lastly, insert the working end beside its own standing part (3). Follow the initial lead around to double, triple, or quadruple the knot (4).

**3**

**4**

# TURK'S HEAD
## 5L x 4B

Any Turk's head knot that has a number of leads and
bights which differ by only one is known as a "square"
Turk's head; and this one is a versatile knot, being
equally suitable for use as a mundane whipping on a
rope's end (to prevent it fraying) or for some more
ornamental purpose.

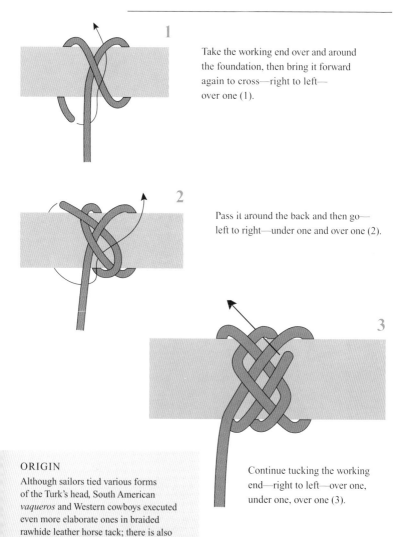

**1**

Take the working end over and around
the foundation, then bring it forward
again to cross—right to left—
over one (1).

**2**

Pass it around the back and then go—
left to right—under one and over one (2).

**3**

Continue tucking the working
end—right to left—over one,
under one, over one (3).

## ORIGIN

Although sailors tied various forms
of the Turk's head, South American
*vaqueros* and Western cowboys executed
even more elaborate ones in braided
rawhide leather horse tack; there is also
evidence of the knot in the tombs of
ancient Egyptian pharaohs.

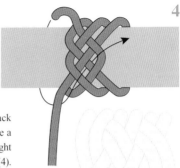

Take the end down, around, and back
to the front of the work, to make a
penultimate locking tuck—left to right
once more—under, over, under, over (4).

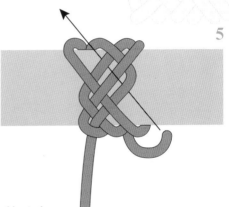

Then make a final locking tuck—
right to left—under, over, under,
over (5, 6). Place the working end
alongside its standing part to double
or triple the ply of this knot.

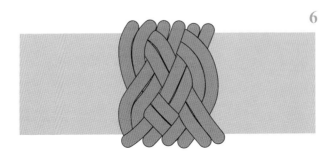

# OVAL MAT

Made in ornamental cord, pairs of this knot could make epaulettes for the uniforms of marching bands. Tied in rope, it becomes a doormat. It may be tied directly onto a flat surface, by hand, with no artificial aids; but early efforts to do so can be made easier by pinning it onto a thick cork or polystyrene ceiling tile or similar baseboard.

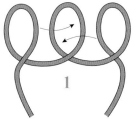

Form a trio of overhand loops and interlace them exactly as shown (1).

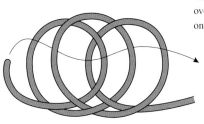

Tuck the working end—left to right—over one, under one, over two, under one, over one (2).

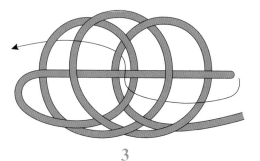

Bring the same end back—right to left—tucking over one, under one, over two (crossing over itself at this point), under one, over one, under one (3).

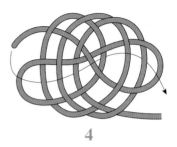

**4**

Return—left to right—with a locking
tuck going over, under, over, under,
over, under, over, under, over (4).

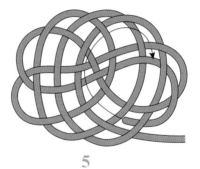

**5**

Bring the working end around to lie beside
its standing part and, following the initial
lead, double the ply of this knot (5, 6).

**6**

# OCEAN BRAID MAT

This wholly symmetrical mat is simpler to tie than the oval mat (*see pages 92–93*) and may be achieved without using pins and board.

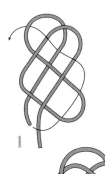

Start with the layout shown, and take the working end around counterclockwise, tucking over one, under two, over one, under one, over one, under one (1).

Then make a final locking tuck, over, under, over, under, over (2).

Bring the working end and the standing part together, parallel (3). Double or triple the mat, as desired (4).

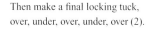

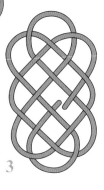

This bowline is less likely to come apart, if shaken or tugged spasmodically, than its European counterpart, and has a slick trip-&-tighten tying method. In the 20th century it was known to merchant seamen as a Panama bowline, apparently from its use in the lines of ships taken through the canal of that name.

Make an uncompleted overhand knot (1).

Tuck the working end up through it, in a locking tuck that goes over, under, over (2).

Pull on—or load—the standing part, and the initial layout capsizes into the final knot form (3).

Further tightening removes the familiar bowline or sheet bend appearance to create a compact three-part crown (4).

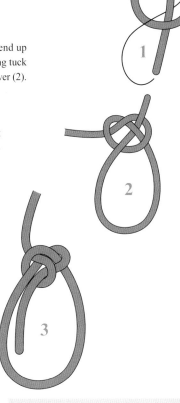

### ORIGIN

There is evidence that this unorthodox but handy variant of the common bowline (*see page 30*) was used by a tribe of Arctic Inuits to start rawhide lashings toward the end of the 18th century.

# ICHABOD KNOT

A sliding loop or noose like this was employed once upon a time to snare animals and birds for food. It will also start a package lashing, or act as a hitch to rail, ring, spar, or post. Pass the standing end through the loop and a running Ichabod knot results, which (like the running bowline, *see page 33*) falls loose when the load is removed.

Form a bight in the end of the line and take the working end around the standing part to create a loop (1).

Now pass the working end twice around both loop legs (2, 3).

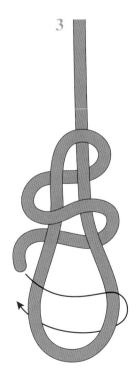

ORIGIN

This sliding loop knot was reportedly tied as a hangman's noose at the old Newcastle jail, Delaware, in the early half of the 20th century, but was probably used more prosaically by local farmers to tether livestock.

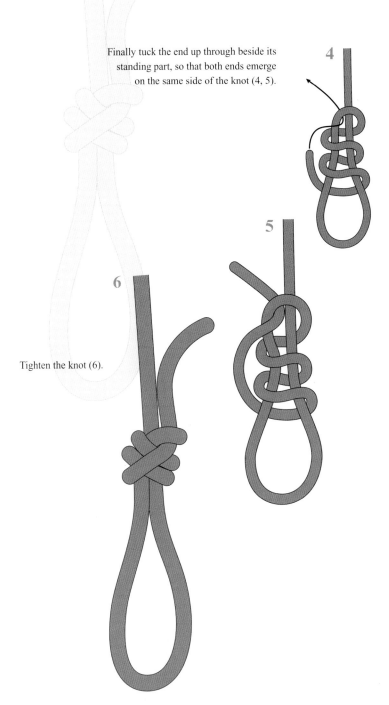

Finally tuck the end up through beside its standing part, so that both ends emerge on the same side of the knot (4, 5).

**4**

**5**

**6**

Tighten the knot (6).

# GIBBET KNOT

This alternative to the Ichabod knot (*see pages 96–97*) can be used in exactly the same way; but, given the immense variety of modern cordage, one knot may work better than the other in some materials. Such sliding loops are useful as reusable hitches, to start lashings, and for packages.

Make a bight in the end of the line and then take the working end around the standing part, as shown, to form a loop (1).

Wrap the end three times around both loop legs (2, 3).

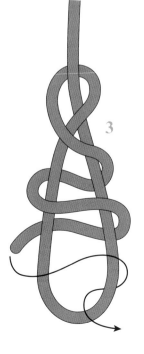

## ORIGIN

A gibbet was a gallows from which executed criminals were suspended, so the name of this knot implies that—like the Ichabod knot (*see pages 96–97*)— it too was once a hangman's noose.

Pass the end through the loop, before tucking it up beside the standing part so that both ends emerge on the same side of the knot (4, 5).

Tighten the knot (6).

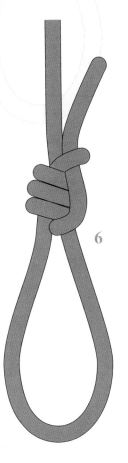

# SANSOME BEND

Knots are like tools: bodgers use and misuse (or abuse) the same few for every task that comes to hand. Craftspeople take the time and trouble to acquire a lot, so as always to have available precisely what is required for the best result. This forgotten knot is worth a try when conventional bends prove unreliable in slick, stretchy, or troublesome stuff. It is a tenacious bend and can even remain tight when it is tied in modern bungee cords (shock elastics).

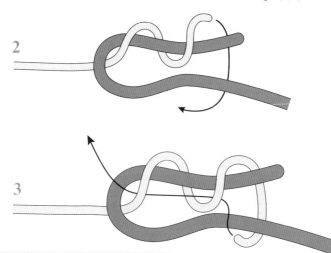

Make a bight in one line and tuck the other working end through to wrap twice around the inert end of the bight (1, 2).

## ORIGIN

Englishman Malcolm Hughes learned this knot from his grandfather, Philip Sansome, who claimed to have used it for joining lengths of elastic when he was a young man in the weaving trade at Loughborough, in the English county of Leicester, around 1845.

Pass the working end around both bight legs and then tuck it back, through its own two wrapping turns, to emerge on the opposite side of the knot from its own standing part (3, 4).

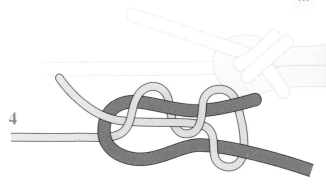

**4**

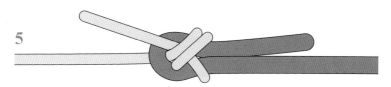

**5**

Then tighten the knot (5).

The evolution of knots reveals a mean streak: once a layout that works manifests itself, it recurs. See how similar the Bugaboo bend is— a knot found by Canadian climber Robert Chisnall, tied in a discarded sling, during an expedition to the Bugaboo Mountains in the summer of 1982.

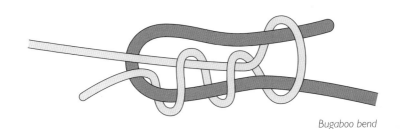

*Bugaboo bend*

One particular use for a sheepshank (other than as a shortening) is to bridge and temporarily safeguard a weak or damaged portion of rope by placing the strain on the other two legs; in this case it is vital that both ends of the knot are secure. There are numerous ways to achieve this, three of which are described here.

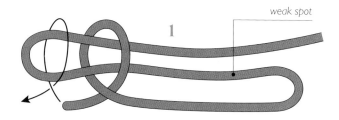

weak spot

1

Method 1: double the retaining loop at each end, to form a clove hitch (1, 2).

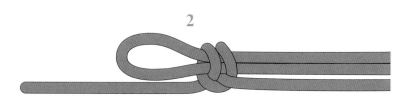

2

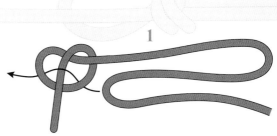

Method 2: form an uncompleted overhand knot, as shown, and insert a locking tuck—under, over, under—by pulling the loop through it (1, 2).

Method 3: tie a double overhand knot with the working end around the loop (1, 2).

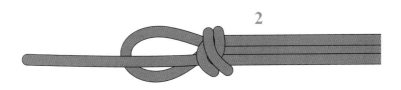

Caution: use this last version only when the load is light or virtually non-existent, and the stuff in which it is tied has plenty of friction. Because, while it is the neatest and apparently the most secure of the three methods, a heavy pull on both ends will undo this knot.

# GROUND LINE HITCH

This secure alternative to the clove hitch (*see pages 25 and 26*) has been used afloat on nets to trawl the seas of the world for cod, and ashore as a picket-line hitch by cavalry. It is a versatile knot that can be employed whenever a line must be attached to an anchorage point to withstand a right-angled load.

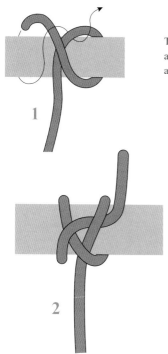

**1**

Take a turn around the rail, ring, or spar, and lay the working end diagonally across the standing part of the line (1).

Pass the end down around the back and bring it up at the front once more, tucking—left to right—over one, under one (2).

**2**

Alternatively, do not pull the end through completely, but leave the draw-loop protruding for quick release (3).

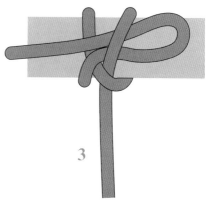

**3**

Small and flexible articles attached by means of a single loop to a ring (for example, key fobs or zipper tags) can be lost if excessive wear due to friction causes them to break. Adding an extra couple of knot parts reduces the load on each by one-third. There are two ways in which to achieve this.

Method 1: tuck the fob or tag up through the ring and then down behind itself, in effect tying a half hitch in the doubled line (1, 2).

Method 2: tuck the fob or tag through its own loop, and then arrange the result as shown (1, 2).

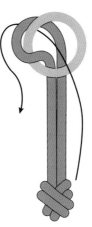

## ORIGIN

The peerless American knotting author and illustrator Clifford Warren Ashley became interested in the problem of reinforcing ring hitches when a watch guard that he prized began to show signs of wear. He published these two tying methods in 1944.

# IMPROVISED HACKAMORE KNOT

Knotted rope halters tied over and around the heads of horses as *ad hoc* bridles to tether, lead, train, and ride them have as their basis one of several hackamore knots. These customarily have twin loops emerging from one end of the knot, with a single loop and two long ends at the other end. This version is easier to tie than traditional models.

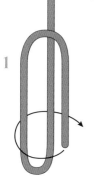

1

Fold the rope into three parts, as if to begin a sheepshank (*see pages 23, 24*). Wrap one end around to enclose both legs of the adjacent bight and its own standing part (1, 2).

2

Wrap the end a second time around all three standing parts, then pull a drawloop through beneath the turns to complete a slipped double overhand knot (3).

3

## ORIGIN

Makeshift headstalls, bridles, or harnesses tied in rope have been around for as long as humankind has been catching, breaking, and riding horses. This is just one of many such age-old cordage contrivances.

Adjust the resulting loops and
ends to the required length,
then tighten the knot (4).

4

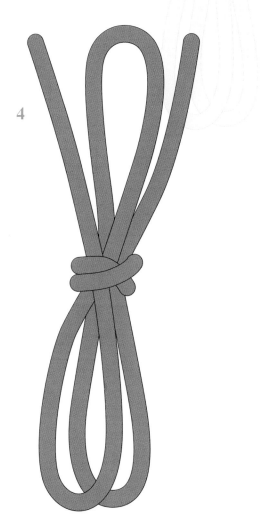

Tying this knot (pronounced "fee-ah-door") may not go right every time; so if at first you don't succeed, tie, tie, and tie again. It forms the basis for a horse's bridle or headstall. Only the knot is described here, its application to the horse's head—with brow-band, ear loops, and cheek straps, plus attachments for bit and reins—being a matter for separate tuition from an experienced instructor.

Double a length of rope or cord, double it again, and temporarily seize the resulting four parts together with adhesive drafting tape or twine (1, 2).

Bend the single upper loop down, and similarly seize it to the two loose ends (3).

Lift up the single loop and tuck the two loose ends down through it, exactly as shown (4).

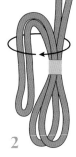

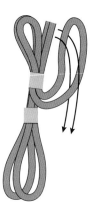

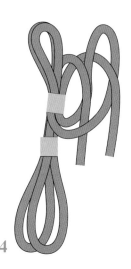

## ORIGIN

This classic knot is of Spanish origin, but following Theodore Roosevelt's success as commander of a volunteer force of "rough riders" in the Spanish-American War of 1898, the name was deliberately changed by western U.S. horsemen to the Theodore knot—a term still used today.

Now turn the work around, then tuck each
end in turn up through its respective loop
(5, 6). The tying is now completed.

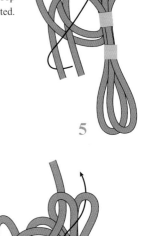

Carefully, so as not to disturb the
positions of the various knotted
parts, remove each tape (the upper
one first), and painstakingly coax
the knot into its final form (7)
before tightening it.

5

6

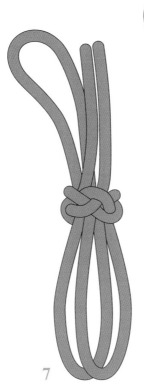

7

# HORSE DEALER'S HITCH

Tethering a horse is rarely as simple as it appears when Hollywood cowboys dismount outside the saloon or general store and, after a single twirl of reins around a crude wooden hitching rail, leave their mounts unattended. A knot that can be deftly tied in rope or rein, and which a perverse animal cannot easily undo with its teeth, is usually required. This one comes recommended.

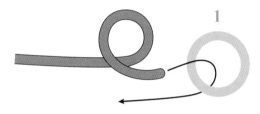

**1**

Pass the end of the halter rope through the ring, at the same time twisting an overhand loop into the standing part (1).

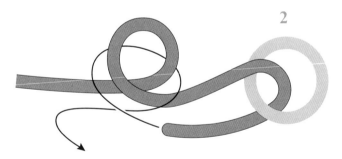

**2**

Bring the end of the rope back and take it clockwise around the initial loop (2).

## ORIGIN

North of England knot tyer A. P. Bloomer was taught this knot in the first half of the 20th century by a horse dealer. Since then, he claims, he has tied it in the dark, in the wet, sometimes with an argumentative horse on the other end, and has never known it to slip.

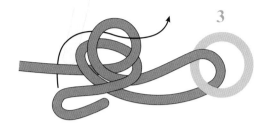

Then tuck a bight beneath the standing part of the rope and up through the original loop from back to front (3, 4).

Tighten the knot (5). To undo it, simply tug on the end to pull out the drawloop.

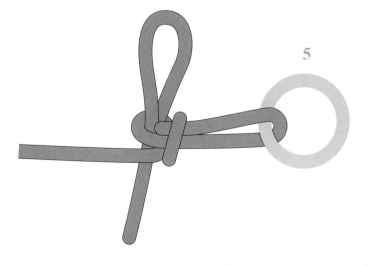

# ARMS-AKIMBO LANYARD KNOT

Single-strand lanyard knots like this one can be tied in the finest of threads or thick cord, but something in between—which shows the knot's distinctive outline and texture—is ideal. This knot was once recommended for the cord that secured a gentleman's monocle to the lapel of his jacket, and today would do just as well to suspend reading spectacles around the neck. You can also make a series of these knots into a bracelet, anklet, or necklace.

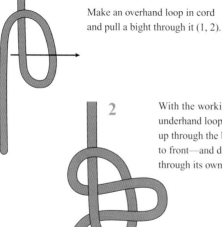

Make an overhand loop in cord and pull a bight through it (1, 2).

With the working end, form an underhand loop, then lead the end up through the bight—from back to front—and down again to tuck through its own loop (3, 4).

## ORIGIN
The name derives from the knot's resemblance to a person standing, hands on hips and elbows stuck out sideways.

Tighten the knot gradually, maintaining its symmetry, to achieve the distinctive two faces (5, 6).

**4**

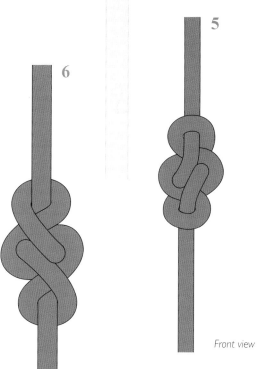

**5**

*Front view*

**6**

*Rear view*

# CHINESE CLOVERLEAF KNOT

Like the preceding lanyard knot (*see pages 112–113*), this
is purely decorative, but is intriguing to tie for its own sake.

Make a bight in the cord, then bring
the end around to tuck a second
bight—over, under—through the
first one (1).

Repeat the process (2).

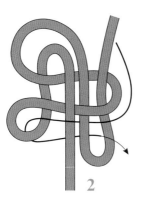

Then, continuing clockwise, take the
working end and insert a locking tuck
(inward) over, under, over, over, to
return (outward) under, under, under,
over. The resulting layout tightens
into a triangular knot form, with three
optional loops, for a neck lanyard (3).

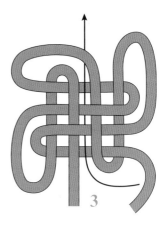

## ORIGIN

This is one of the simpler knots from a
family of increasingly elaborate Chinese
ornamental knots, used to adorn clothing
or attach amulets and other valued items.
Generations of Chinese children, in
common with their Western counterparts,
have been told the clover is a lucky plant.

Otherwise, before tightening the knot,
tuck the working end up through the
center of the knot, as shown (4).

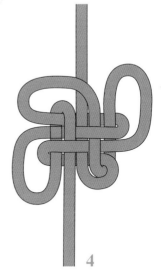

**4**

Then tighten carefully to create a handsome
square-shaped and solid knot (5).

**5**

# MYSTIC KNOT

This knot, which has Buddhist connotations and is also known as the Pan Chang knot, makes an eye-catching loop in the end of any neck lanyard. It is easier to tie if each stage is pinned onto a cork or polystyrene tile or board, rather than attempted directly by hand on a flat surface, although this is not essential.

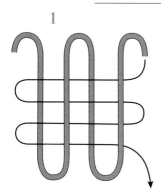

**1**

Arrange the first two interlaced layers, as shown, with one working end (1).

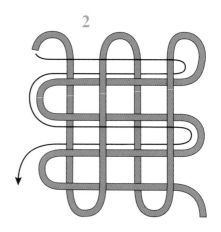

**2**

Then, with the other end, create reciprocal bights (2, 3).

## ORIGIN

According to the Chinese knotting writer Lydia Chen, the mystic or Pan Chang knot is one of the eight Buddhist Treasures, its convolutions being a tangible reminder of the cyclical nature of all existence, which is one of the basic precepts in Chinese Buddhism.

**3**

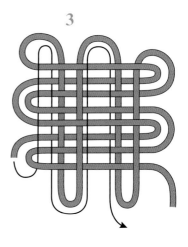

During tightening, which must be done cautiously so as not to distort the slack knot, the seemingly two-dimensional layout separates into an upper and lower layer, forming the two faces of the finished knot (4).

**4**

The primary bottom loop is indispensable, if the knot is part of a lanyard, but the six secondary lateral loops may be left open or tightened.

# BLIMP KNOT

After the preceding two knots, this one is easy. It is another simple embellishment for a lanyard, which resembles the zeppelin bend (*see pages 66–67*), but is smaller and softer, hence its whimsical name (a "blimp" being a light, non-rigid, often tethered aircraft or large balloon).

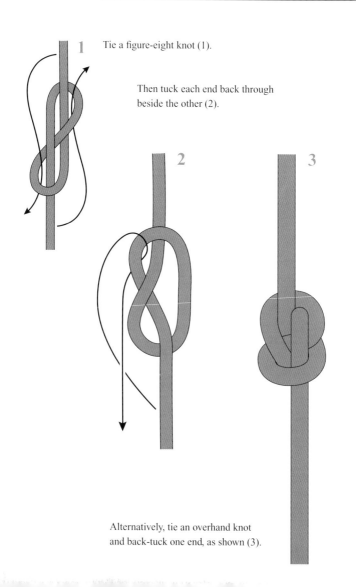

Tie a figure-eight knot (1).

Then tuck each end back through beside the other (2).

Alternatively, tie an overhand knot and back-tuck one end, as shown (3).

# INNOVATIVE KNOTS

*"Given a piece of string, man will find some new way of tying a knot with it."*

CAPTAIN PAUL HARRISON, 1964

New knots are being devised or discovered all the time, but to be assured of a welcome, any newcomer needs to be in some way superior to those knots already in use. The knots in this section have all surfaced within the past couple of decades—or, perhaps, reappeared after a period of neglect— but it may be another 20 years before any one of them becomes an established favorite.

# INTRODUCTION

The legacy bequeathed to us by the ancients and by old-time sailormen, according to the prolific knotting writer Geoffrey Budworth, is certainly not all there is to know about knotting. New knots are invented or encountered every year, while old and neglected ones (perhaps viewed with disfavor by previous generations, for whom they behaved poorly in the cordage then available) are resurrected, rehabilitated, and found to work reliably in modern synthetic materials.

There are knotting devotees who argue that knots cannot be "invented," but—like scientific laws—can only be discovered. A more realistic assessment is perhaps that by John Smith of Surrey, England, who (writing in *Knotting Matters,* in July 1989) pointed out that some knots undoubtedly result from knowledge and skill purposefully applied to achieve a specific outcome. Such knots are surely invented (or at least developed) by the individuals who create them. Other knots come about by accident, through fiddling fingers and curious minds. Thirdly, there is the "Aha!" experience, when some serendipitous combination of turns and tucks, in suitable cordage, is perceived by an alert individual to be an innovative piece of knotting. Smith summed up his three-sided hypothesis as Invention, Accident, or Observation.

Innovative knots must ultimately be assessed by criteria that define fitness of purpose, just as for traditional knots, namely: a form readily learned and taught; ease of tying and untying; adequate strength and security; one or more desirable qualities; and a broad range of applications. The knotting writer and researcher Pieter van de Griend summarizes all of this as "Survival of the Simplest," although the term "simple" may seem an understatement when learning (say) one of the "exploding" knots by Peter Suber included in this section, or Olivier Peron's corkscrew knot.

*Exploding clove hitch*

# Miller's Knot

Binding knots for the necks of sacks need to be quickly applied, be secure without jamming, and be just as easily untied. When binding a hard and unyielding item (such as a hose on a faucet), use soft and stretchy cord for the best effect; on a soft foundation (such as a sack), use hard stuff that will bite into it.

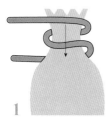

Take the working end twice around the sack's neck and bring the standing part diagonally across the other inert part (1, 2).

**1**

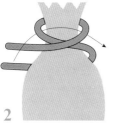

Tuck the working end as shown (3).

**2**

Pull on both ends to tighten the knot (4).

**3**

### ORIGIN
The miller's knot dates back to the days of windmills, when grain and seed (measured in archaic bushels and pecks) were ground for staple foods such as bread and cattle feed, and were then bagged up by the miller into sacks.

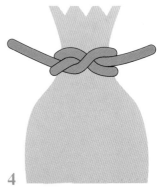

**4**

# Bracelet binding

For those occasions when some ornamentation is desirable, the extra effort taken to tie this knot (also known as the sack knot) is repaid by the neat four-part diamond crown that results.

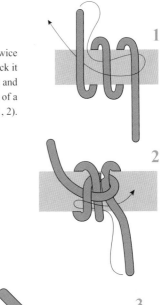

Wrap the working end twice around the object, then tuck it beneath the two inert turns and beneath itself in the form of a half hitch (1, 2).

Tuck the other end in the same manner (3), then work the knot snug and tight (4).

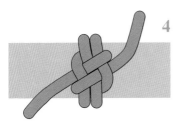

## ORIGIN

Sack knots of several different sorts, like this one, were used in previous centuries, when various granular or powdered dry goods were simply bagged in flax, jute, or hessian sacks.

# JULIE'S HITCH

This hitch has proved to be handy when an anchorage point (such as an overhead rail or a trailer axle) is beyond comfortable reach, in which case the doubled end of a line may be thrown or otherwise passed around it. However, the actual knot has to be tied closer to hand.

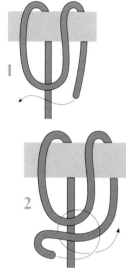

Double the end of the line and loop, and pass the resulting bight over the distant anchorage point. Take the working end around the standing part and tuck it through the bight, from front to back (1, 2).

Tuck the working end through the bight a second time (3), and lead it down beside the standing part (4).

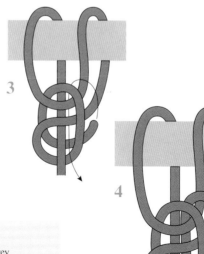

## ORIGIN

The knot is named after Geoffrey Budworth's younger daughter Julie, who discovered it for herself in 1974 when she was just nine years old. It was included in his *Knot Book* in 1983.

Carefully tighten the knot, so that the twin loops compensate for an uneven load by feeding one into the other (5).

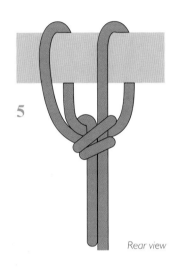

5

*Rear view*

6

It is advisable to secure the working end to the standing part by means of a bowline or other backup knot (6).

*Front view*

# FRUSTRATOR

This binding is kin to the constrictor knot (*see pages 47–51*). Not only is it secure in use, but it also resists attempts to undo it (hence its name). It works best when tied in the bight, although it is not impossible to make this knot with an end.

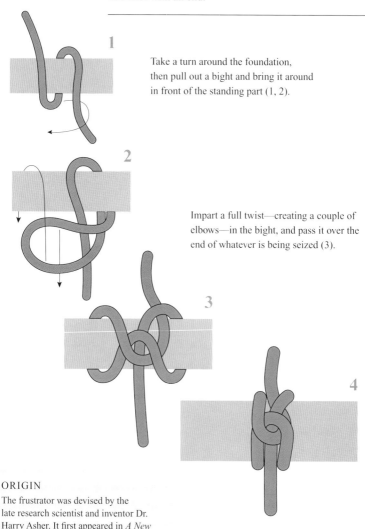

**1**

Take a turn around the foundation, then pull out a bight and bring it around in front of the standing part (1, 2).

**2**

Impart a full twist—creating a couple of elbows—in the bight, and pass it over the end of whatever is being seized (3).

**3**

**4**

## ORIGIN

The frustrator was devised by the late research scientist and inventor Dr. Harry Asher. It first appeared in *A New System of Knotting—Volume II*, written by him and published in 1986 by the International Guild of Knot Tying.

Pull on both ends to tighten the knot (4). Once it jams, the ends may be cut short.

# Ring hitch doubled

You can use this hitch to join two rings, eyes, or swivels by means of a continuous sling or strop. Despite the fact that it looks difficult to accomplish, it is actually quite easy to tie and may be done in a variety of stuff, ranging from webbing to cord and tape, on any scale.

Take the end of the sling through one of the rings, then pass it through itself, thereby creating a simple ring hitch (1).

Next, pass the remaining bight through the second ring, beneath the crossing loop, and completely over the first ring (2).

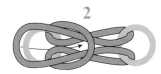

Tighten the working bight behind the initial ring hitch to interlock the various parts of the knot (3, 4).

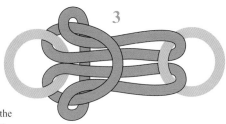

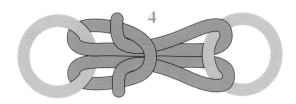

## ORIGIN
This hitch may date back to medieval times, although it was recently rediscovered by Joe McNicholas of Pennsylvania.

# CLINGING CLARA HITCH

This hitch was designed to withstand a longitudinal pull upon a cord that is attached to a hawser-laid rope. It has two distinct forms.

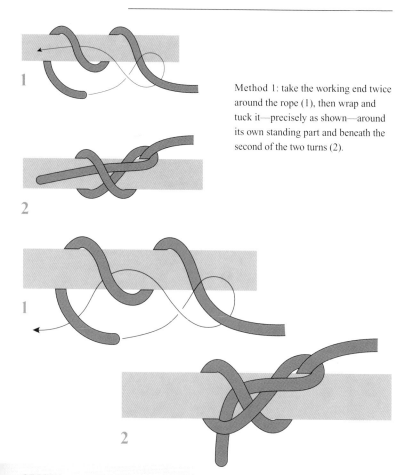

Method 1: take the working end twice around the rope (1), then wrap and tuck it—precisely as shown—around its own standing part and beneath the second of the two turns (2).

## ORIGIN

This hitch (and the two derivatives that follow) is another innovative knot, first published in 1986, from the active mind and fingers of the late Dr. Harry Asher.

Method 2: start as if tying method 1, but finally tuck the working end beneath two knot parts, rather than one (1, 2).

# QUEEN CLARA HITCH

This superior version of the clinging Clara hitch (*see opposite*) appears to be able to withstand greater strains on its inherent strength and security; but, like all innovative knots, only continual use over time will reveal whether or not it deserves its title.

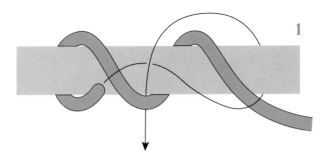

Wrap the working end twice around the hawser, and then bring it back beyond its own standing part and around the rope once more, but in the opposite direction (1).

Tuck the working end—over two, under one—as shown (2).

Dr. Harry Asher concocted this hitch to withstand a longitudinal pull on a smooth spar and successfully demonstrated it in 1986, on the display stand of the International Guild of Knot Tyers at the annual Boat Show, held in London's Earls Court exhibition hall, when it coped with a pull toward the narrow end of a billiard cue.

1

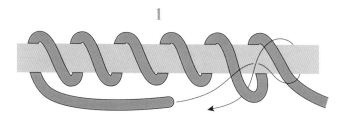

Lead the working end at least six turns around the foundation, then bring it back beyond its own standing part and around the rope once more, but in the opposite direction (1).

2

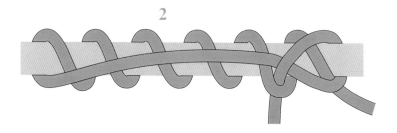

Tuck the working end—over two, under one—as shown (2), as for the Queen Clara hitch (*see page 129*).

Hoisting scaffold poles, a boat mast, or other smooth, heavy lengths requires a hitch with friction to withstand a sustained longitudinal pull, yet it ought to be readily applied and just as easily cast off again. This hitch is one of many with those very qualities.

Wrap the working end tightly, in a downward direction, six to eight times around the object to be lifted (1).

Then bring the end up and around the standing part (2).

Lastly, take it down once more, and apply a restraining half hitch (3).

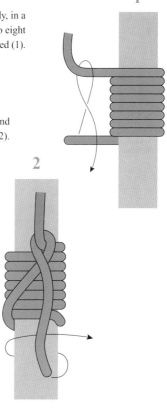

**1**

**2**

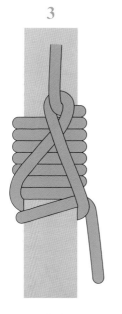

**3**

## ORIGIN

This lifting hitch is similar to those featured in his excellent *A Fresh Approach to Knotting and Ropework* by Charles Warner, published in 1992.

# PEACE KNOT

This unusual fixed-loop knot replaces the bowline and other such knots, if these are likely to jam and become hard to untie, with the useful property that it falls apart (no further untying required) when the drawloop is removed.

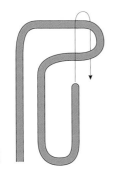

Make a bight in the standing part of the line and enclose it in another bight made with the working end (1, 2).

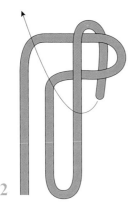

Create a diagonal crossing with the end, tucking it down behind the incomplete knot and bringing it—from back to front—out through the large loop (3, 4).

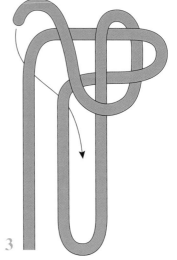

## ORIGIN

The Faroese knotting writer/researcher Pieter van de Griend thought up this knot while working on the waterfront at Terneuzen, and published it in 1986. He and other seamen used it, tied in ⅘ inch (20 mm) diameter nylon rope, to hoist mooring lines from ship to jetty.

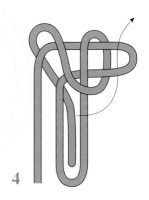

**4**

Finally, tuck a drawloop up through the initial bight (5) and tighten the knot (6).

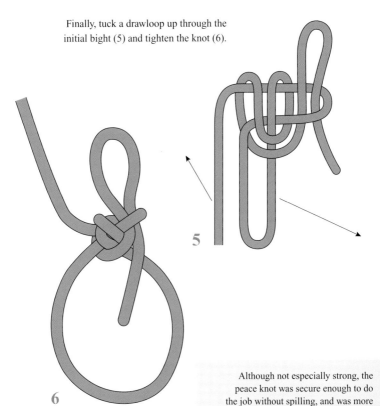

**5**

**6**

Although not especially strong, the peace knot was secure enough to do the job without spilling, and was more easily untied than bowlines, which jammed when heavily loaded (or so the longshoremen forcibly complained).

# BUBBLE KNOT

The odd name gives no clue to the use of this knot,
which is as a kind of button-&-loop fastening that may
be applied and cast off easily in many varied situations.

In a short length of cord tie a
figure-eight knot, then take one
end up through and around the
knot to tuck as shown (1).

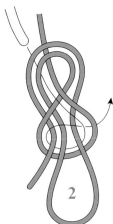

Introduce the rope that the fastening will
serve, tucking and tying as illustrated (2, 3).

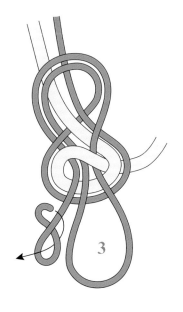

## ORIGIN

This knot appeared in issue no. 403
(July 2000) of the British monthly
magazine *Practical Boat Owner*, and
subsequently in issue no. 74 (March
2002) of *Knotting Matters*.

Lastly, add a figure-eight knot (or an Ashley's stopper knot) to the cord end that lies alongside the loop and tighten the entire contrivance (4).

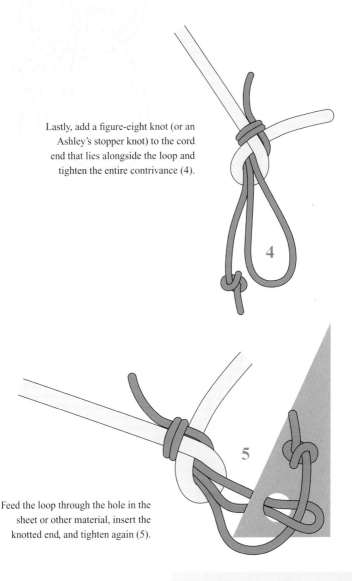

Feed the loop through the hole in the sheet or other material, insert the knotted end, and tighten again (5).

It was dreamed up by Michael Collis, who used it as a quick and easy means of swapping the leads or sheets from one jib sail to another. He reported that the knot had never shaken loose (not even in a force six across the North Sea).

# LOCKING LOOP

This knot is one of several slide-&-grip knots that can be shifted by hand to adjust the size of the loop, but which (when loaded) locks firmly into place by creating an abrupt bend in the standing part of the line.

Form a bight in the end of the line (1).

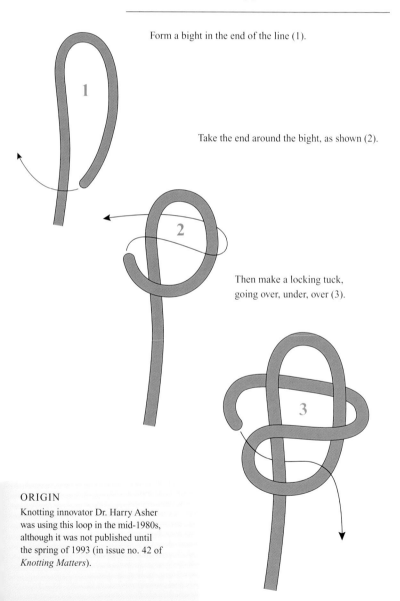

Take the end around the bight, as shown (2).

Then make a locking tuck, going over, under, over (3).

ORIGIN

Knotting innovator Dr. Harry Asher was using this loop in the mid-1980s, although it was not published until the spring of 1993 (in issue no. 42 of *Knotting Matters*).

Tighten the knot just enough to secure it, while still letting it shift as required (4).

Add a drawloop, tucking the working end back alongside itself. This knot has two distinct faces that reveal the mechanism by which it works (5, 6).

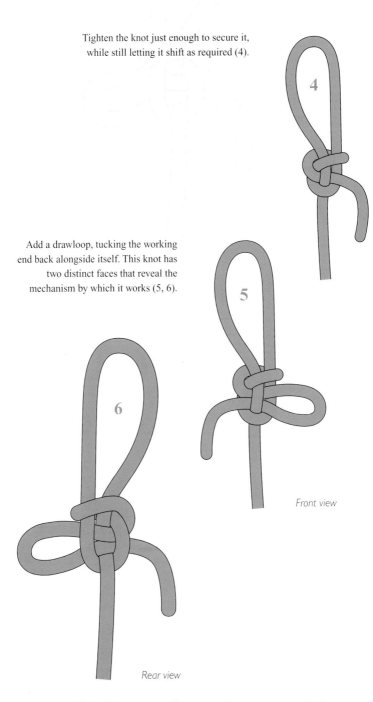

*Front view*

*Rear view*

# SLIP-&-NIP NOOSE

This noose not only makes a quick fastening to a rail, post, or spar, but (if tightened) also withstands a longitudinal pull (without the usual numerous wrapping turns that are characteristic of such hitches). It incorporates a useful pinching mechanism, whereby pushing the two enclosing bights closer together tightens the knot, but separating them makes it easier to untie.

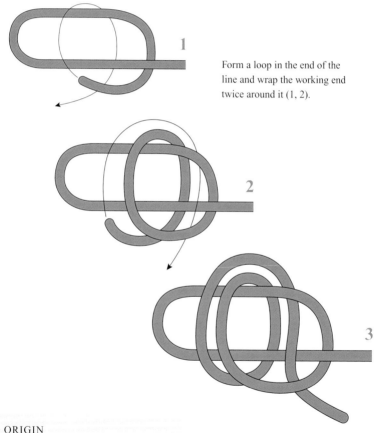

Form a loop in the end of the line and wrap the working end twice around it (1, 2).

ORIGIN

Dr. Brooks A. Mick, M.D., of Findlay, Ohio, published this loop knot in issue no. 8 (summer 1984) of *Knotting Matters*.

Tuck the end down between the standing part of the line and the initial turn (3).

**4**

Tighten the knot (4), and push the
two enclosing loops together (5).

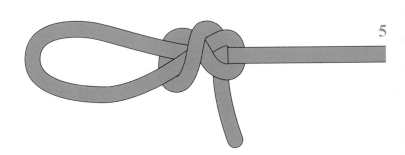

**5**

# THE INNOMIKNOT

This versatile, general-purpose, heavy-duty hitch can be tied in the bight. From tethering an animal to overcoming a wilderness challenge, its applications are many.

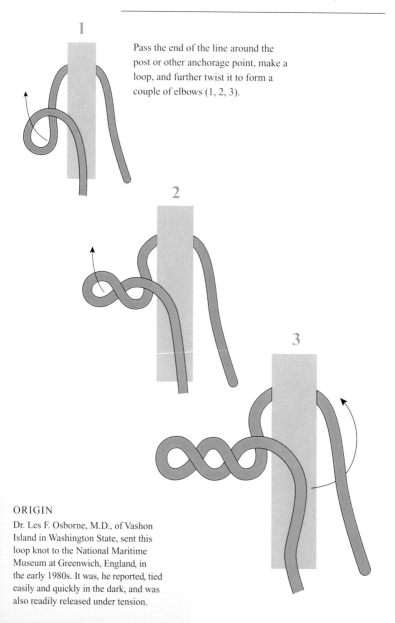

Pass the end of the line around the post or other anchorage point, make a loop, and further twist it to form a couple of elbows (1, 2, 3).

## ORIGIN

Dr. Les F. Osborne, M.D., of Vashon Island in Washington State, sent this loop knot to the National Maritime Museum at Greenwich, England, in the early 1980s. It was, he reported, tied easily and quickly in the dark, and was also readily released under tension.

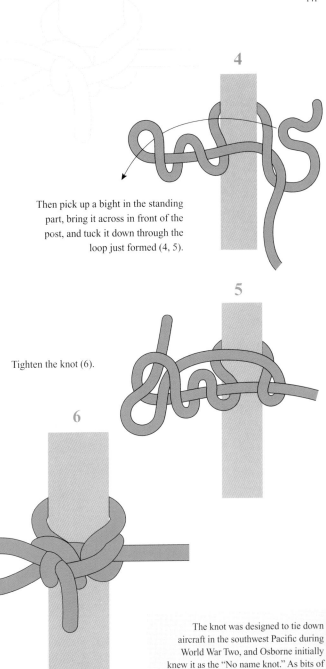

**4**

Then pick up a bight in the standing part, bring it across in front of the post, and tuck it down through the loop just formed (4, 5).

**5**

Tighten the knot (6).

**6**

The knot was designed to tie down aircraft in the southwest Pacific during World War Two, and Osborne initially knew it as the "No name knot." As bits of anatomy without a name are said to be "innominate," Geoffrey Budworth suggested (and Osborne agreed) that it made sense to call this the innomiknot.

# Exploding clove hitch

Most so-called "slipped" knots, which incorporate a quick-release drawloop, nevertheless require some untying after the loop has been freed. Shoelaces are an everyday example. This knot—in common with the five that follow—falls apart (or "explodes") completely when the drawloop is freed. The Lapp and peace knots (*see pages 76 and 132–133 respectively*) also share this property.

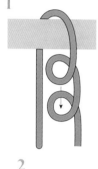

**1**

Take the working end around the anchorage point, and then make a couple of overhand loops in the standing part of the line (1).

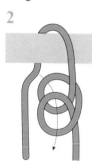

**2**

Overlap the loops, as shown (2), and pull a bight from the working end through them (3).

**3**

Then tighten the knot (4). To release, tug on the short end.

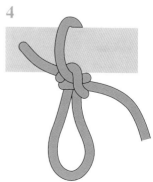

**4**

### ORIGIN

This knot was devised by Peter Suber of Richmond, Indiana, and it featured as "Knot of the Month" in *Boating* magazine in October 1999.

# EXPLODING FIGURE-EIGHT HITCH

Like the preceding knot (as well as those that follow), this hitch of Peter Suber's is primarily intended by its innovator for use in climbing and outdoor pursuits; and in this connection there are extra subtleties concerned with tying, tightening, and releasing it, not dealt with here. Suber's own far more detailed descriptions and analyses can be found on his Internet website (*see page 205*).

**1**

Take the working end around the anchorage, and then tie a slipped figure-eight knot in the standing part (1).

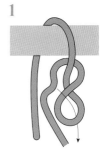

**2**

Pull out a further bight from the working end, and tuck it in turn through the drawloop just formed (2, 3).

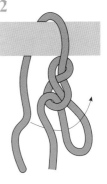

**3**

Carefully tighten the knot, keeping it flat (4).

**4**

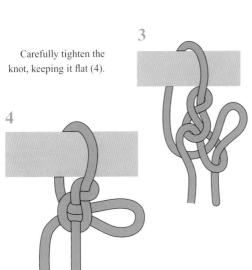

# EXPLODING
# BUTTERFLY HITCH

The figure-eight layout that is apparent during the tying of this knot disappears when it is tightened, and it then acquires the useful quality of becoming a slide-&-lock loop.

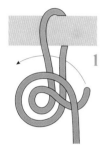

Place a long bight of rope over the post or around the tree that is the chosen anchorage, then form a loop with both parts of the line (1).

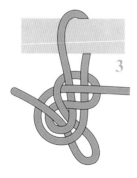

Take the working end around behind the bight, and simply pull a further bight down through the twin loops to form a drawloop (2, 3).

Tighten the knot, taking care to keep it flat (4).

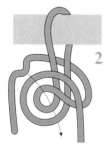

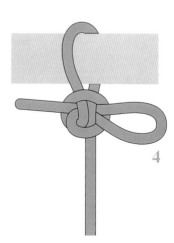

This knot is the favorite (in this series of six "exploding" knots) of the inventor, Peter Suber. It too is a useful slide-&-lock loop.

Pass the working end around the anchorage and lift up a bight within the standing part (1).

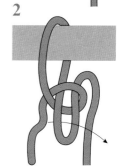

Form an underhand loop with the working end, and fit it in the form of a half hitch over the lower bight in the standing part (2).

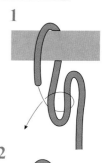

Then pull a bight from the end through the bight beneath the half hitch (3). Tighten the knot, taking care to keep it flat (4).

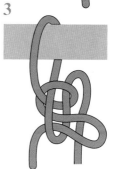

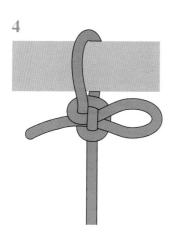

# EXPLODING CHINESE CROWN HITCH

Despite its apparent complexity, this knot (devised, like the five other "exploding" hitches, by Peter Suber) can be tied in seconds.

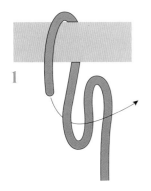

Pass the working end around the anchorage, pick up a bight in the standing part, and tuck the working end through it, as shown (1).

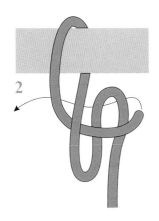

Pass the end around the back of everything, from right to left, and then pull a bight through the original loop (2, 3).

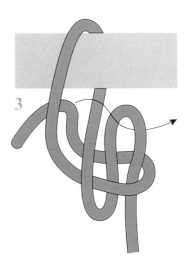

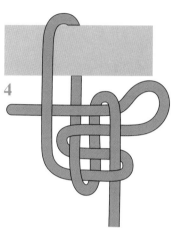

Tighten the whole knot carefully, keeping it flat (4, 5).

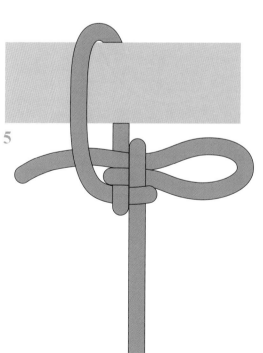

# Exploding double carrick hitch

This is the last of the six super "exploding" knots invented by Peter Suber, from Richmond, Indiana.

---

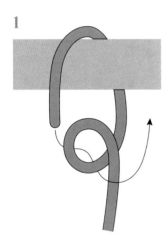

Pass the working end over the anchorage and form an underhand loop in the standing part (1).

Bring the short end, from left to right, beneath the loop and over the standing part (2).

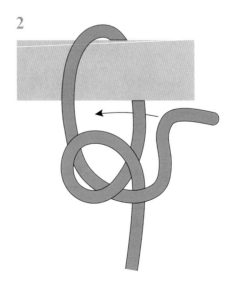

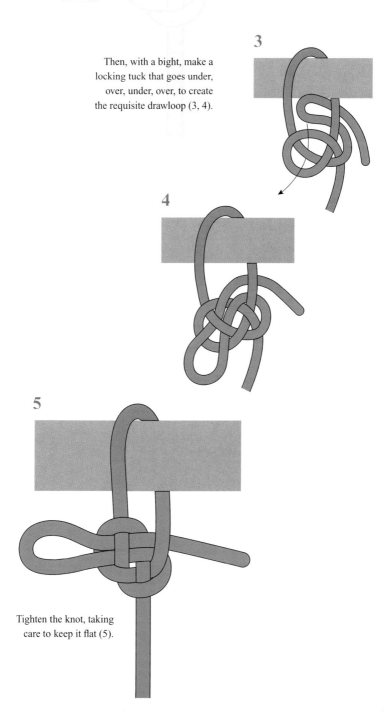

**3**

Then, with a bight, make a locking tuck that goes under, over, under, over, to create the requisite drawloop (3, 4).

**4**

**5**

Tighten the knot, taking care to keep it flat (5).

# CORKSCREW KNOT

It is claimed that this knot is superior to many other climbing knots in rappeling (abseiling) on static or dynamic lines; and that, because it withstands shock loading of various intensities and differing frequencies, it is suited to acrobatic work, tree cutting, et cetera. It can be tied in the bight and released from a distance, limited only by the doubled length of the rope. There are two different methods of tying the corkscrew.

**1**

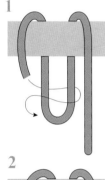

Method 1: lay a longish bight over the anchorage point, then wrap the load end at least three times (no fewer) around it, as shown (1, 2).

**2**

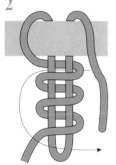

Bring the release end from behind the wrapped bight, then tuck it over the load end and down through the bight to create a drawloop (3). Carefully tighten the knot (4).

**3**

**4**

### ORIGIN

This knot is the progenitor of a family of corkscrew knots devised by the French circus performer Olivier Peron, who published them in a series of booklets in 1998.

Method 2: to equalize the load between a couple of anchorages, double the rope and arrange it around both anchorages, as shown (1).

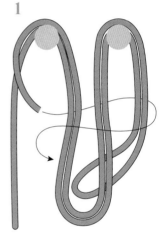

**1**

Wrap the load end as before, then take a turn (in the opposite direction) with the release end, before tucking to create the required drawloop (2).

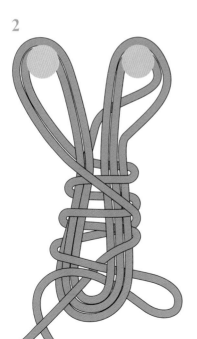

**2**

# KATHERINE'S KNOT

Essentially a "left-handed" sheet bend (that is, one in which the short ends emerge on opposite sides of the knot), this compact little bend has been back-tucked to improve its security.

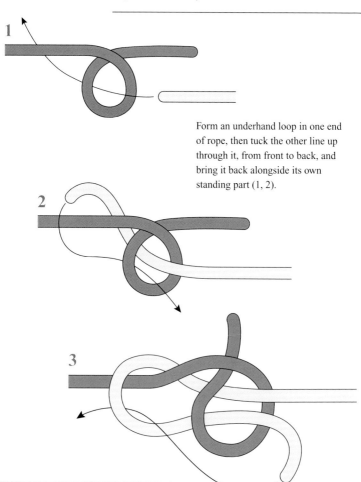

Form an underhand loop in one end of rope, then tuck the other line up through it, from front to back, and bring it back alongside its own standing part (1, 2).

Tuck the working end of the doubled line though its own bight (3, 4).

## ORIGIN

This knot was discovered—or perhaps merely rediscovered—in 1982 by Katherine M. Saunders, of Halesowen in the West Midlands of England, and was published in issue no. 7 of *Knotting Matters*.

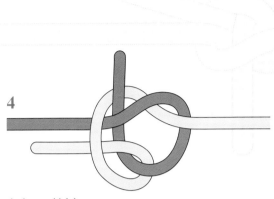

**4**

Tighten the knot, which has
two distinct faces (5, 6).

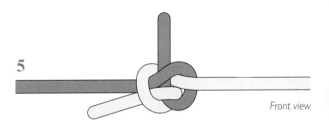

**5**

*Front view*

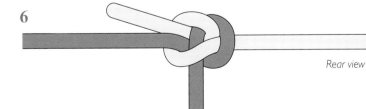

**6**

*Rear view*

# SIMPLE SIMON BEND

You can use this snug and secure bend to join two lines of different thickness when the sheet bend (*see pages 35, 36, and 37*) might prove inadequate.

Make a bight in one line, then tuck the other line up through and around it, as shown (1, 2).

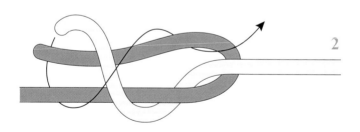

ORIGIN

This is yet another knot (related to the double crossed Simon bend that follows) that first appeared in *A New System of Knotting—Volume I* by Dr. Harry Asher, which was published in 1986 by the International Guild of Knot Tyers.

Bring the working end diagonally across itself, then tuck it one final time, to emerge from the initial bight on the same side as its own standing part (3).

Pull on both legs in order to tighten the knot (4).

# DOUBLE CROSSED SIMON BEND

Like the simple Simon bend (*see pages 154–155*), this knot is intended to join two ropes or cords that are of somewhat dissimilar size or construction.

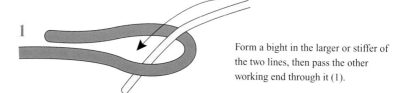

Form a bight in the larger or stiffer of the two lines, then pass the other working end through it (1).

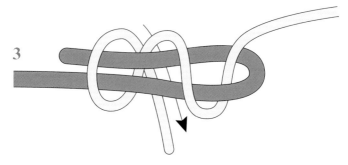

Wrap the end of the lighter line up around the front, down the back, and up around the front once again (2, 3).

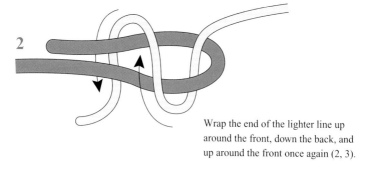

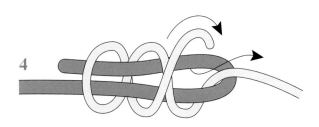

**4**

Now make a return journey, going over at each crossing point and finally tucking the working end up beside its own standing part (4, 5).

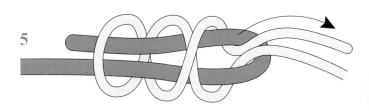

**5**

Pull on both legs of each line to tighten the knot (6).

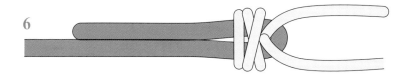

**6**

# Symmetric hawser bend I

This bend is secure in ropes of similar size and construction, and its comparatively gentle curves make it particularly suitable for larger ropes and cables.

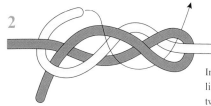

Bend a bight in one line and arrange it to form a couple of loops, as shown (1).

Interweave the working end of the other line: (outward) over one, under two, over two, under one; (return) over three, under one, over one, under one (2, 3).

Tighten the knot (4).

## ORIGIN

Jack Reinmann from Ohio created this secure and good-looking bend (together with the one that follows) and published details of both in issue no. 43 (summer 1993) of *Knotting Matters*.

# Symmetric hawser bend II

This alternative may be superior to the preceding knot, and it can be used in lines that differ somewhat in size and construction.

Make a bight in one rope and twist it to create a couple of elbows (1).

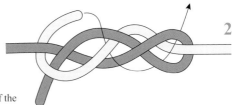

Interweave the working end of the other rope: (outward) over one, under two, over two, under one; (return) over one, under one, over one, under one, over one, under one (2, 3).

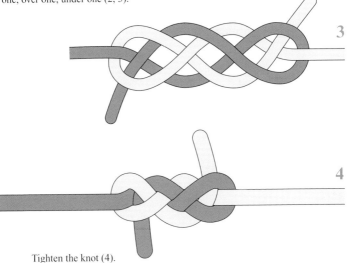

Tighten the knot (4).

# BROACH BEND

Use this compact interwoven bend for smaller diameters than the preceding hawser bends (*see pages 158–159*). Although it requires careful tightening—otherwise it can slip and pull apart in the early stages—it will then hold in slick or slippery materials that cause lesser bends to fail.

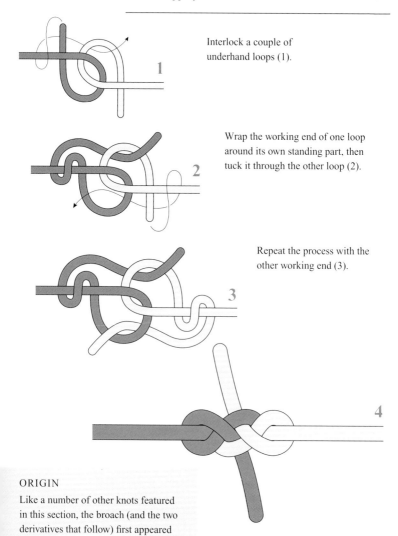

Interlock a couple of underhand loops (1).

Wrap the working end of one loop around its own standing part, then tuck it through the other loop (2).

Repeat the process with the other working end (3).

## ORIGIN

Like a number of other knots featured in this section, the broach (and the two derivatives that follow) first appeared in Dr. Harry Asher's *A New System of Knotting—Volume I*, published in 1986.

Tighten the knot very carefully (4).

For added insurance with ultra-smooth materials that might otherwise do a Houdini and slip free, use this beefed-up broach bend.

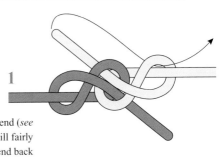

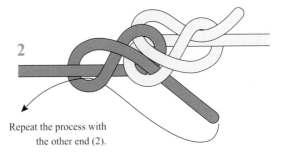

Tie a basic broach bend (*see opposite*) and, while it is still fairly loose, tuck one working end back through the bight surrounding its own standing part, as shown (1).

Repeat the process with the other end (2).

Then tighten the knot (3).

# BROACH LOOP

Bends can often be made into loops (or, conversely, loops can be made into bends) and the broach loop offers a good example of this.

Lay out an uncompleted figure-eight knot in the end of one line (1).

Then, instead of tucking the working end, lead it around and insert it through the lower part, to create the required loop (2).

Wrap and tuck the working end, as shown (3).

Tighten the knot (4).

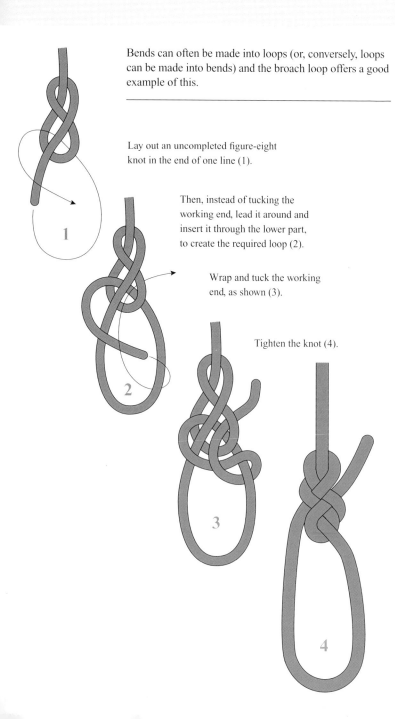

# USEFUL
# MUTATIONS

*"But knotting is merely the application of certain mechanical principles, and a principle itself can hardly become obsolete. As conditions change, new applications are bound to appear."*

<small>CLIFFORD W. ASHLEY, 1944</small>

We may know less than half of all there is to discover about knotting. Not only are new knots still being generated, but long-established ones metamorphose into diverse variants. Far from being a moribund breed, dying from neglect, knots are vibrantly alive and multiplying. Those individuals who have a hand in each new birth or mutation, some of whom are mentioned in this section, add to the useful sum of human knowledge.

# INTRODUCTION

Can you tie a Turk's head? This question is frequently asked of knotting practitioners, to which they can only respond, "Which one?" Because, without wishing to dismiss or put down their questioners, there are hundreds of Turk's head knots of different dimensions and weaves that can easily enough be tied—just five of which are described in this book. Thousands more are theoretically feasible, given enough time, ingenuity, and cord.

From the figure-eight stopper knot evolve more elaborate loops, bends, and hitches. Single loop knots can be adapted to become double, triple, or multiple loop knots, a few of which can be applied in peculiar ways (as a jury mast knot, an improvised horse bridle, or in the form of a chain stitch lashing).

Different tying methods may lead—either intentionally or by chance—to knot variants, while tying material that differs greatly in its construction may result in the emergence of a knot that suits it (see the collared hitch tied in tape or webbing). Knots that are amenable to being tied in flat tape or webbing, and which have already been mentioned, include: the clove hitch; the pole hitch; the buntline hitch; the ossel hitch; the water knot; the ground line hitch; and some ring hitches.

Knots tied a different way, in uncommon cordage, or used for a different purpose can acquire not only another name but another character. The Piwich knot is an adaptation of what sailors would otherwise call an anchor bend; the sheet bend, when executed in woolen yarns, becomes a weaver's knot. And the classic Prusik knot, first created to mend the broken strings of musical instruments, and subsequently used by climbers, becomes in this section a bottle, jar, or jug sling. Mutations are simply a response to altered needs.

*Chain stitch lashing*

# FIGURE-EIGHT LOOP

The advantage of tying a loop in this way—as those who use life-support knots will readily appreciate—is that it may be pulled wide open, from both directions at once, without loss of knot integrity.

---

Tie a figure-eight knot loosely in the standing part of the line (1).

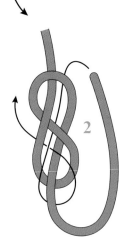

Then insert the working end at the top of the knot, forming a large loop of the required size in the process, and follow the initial lead around until the knot has been duplicated (2, 3, 4).

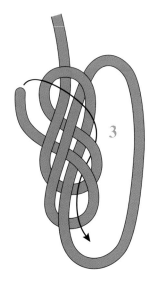

ORIGIN

Dan Lehman of Virginia, a dedicated knot researcher and writer, spotted this knot used as the clip-into loop of top-roping rock climbers, and published it in issue no. 26 of *Knotting Matters* (January 1989).

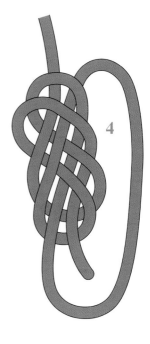

**4**

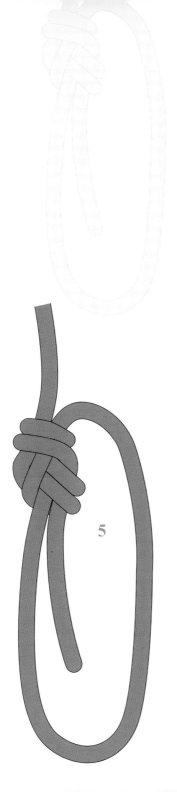

**5**

Tighten the knot methodically
and as neatly as possible (5).

# DOUBLE ANGLER'S LOOP

Twin loops have a number of uses, from improvised chair rescue knots to attachment points for fly-fishing lurers, and this adaptation of the basic angler's loop (*see pages 68–69*) is an ingenious example.

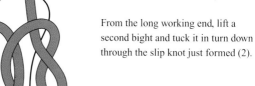

Tie an uncompleted overhand knot and pull a bight through it to form a simple slip knot (1).

**1**

From the long working end, lift a second bight and tuck it in turn down through the slip knot just formed (2).

**2**

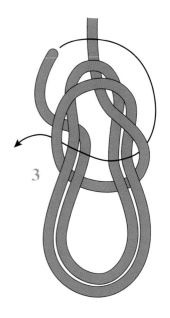

**3**

ORIGIN
This knot first appeared in *A Fresh Approach to Knotting and Ropework* by Charles Warner, which was published in 1992.

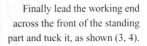

Finally lead the working end across the front of the standing part and tuck it, as shown (3, 4).

**4**

The two distinctive faces (front and rear) of the basic angler's loop are still just recognizable in this bulkier twin-loop version (5, 6).

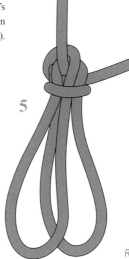

**5**

*Rear view*

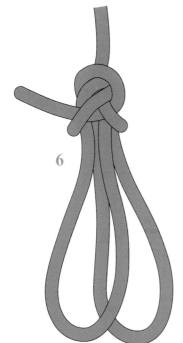

**6**

*Front view*

# BRUMMYCHAM BOWLINE

This double loop is intended to be used only when both ends of the rope are available for tying it. It can, however, be tied in a way similar to that already described for the bowline in the bight (*see pages 72–73*) and may also be made with more than two turns as loops. Indeed, it is a useful method of coiling and hanging up rope for storage.

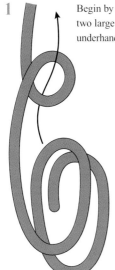

Begin by coiling the rope and, when two large loops appear, add a small underhand loop in the standing part (1).

Tuck the upper bights of both larger loops up through the small loop (2), then pass all of the standing part of the line through these two bights (3).

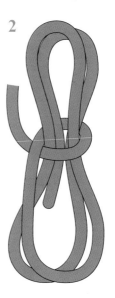

ORIGIN

The active Dr. Harry Asher produced this knot, naming it after his home city of Birmingham (known affectionately to its residents as "Brum") in the West Midlands of England. It first appeared in his *A New System of Knotting* (1986) and later in his *The Alternative Knot Book* (1989).

171

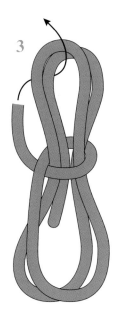

3

Bed the knot down
neatly and tighten it (4).

4

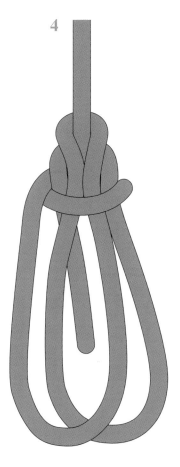

# ROBUST HANDCUFF KNOT

This twin-loop knot is an elaboration of the strangle knot *(see page 46)* and, like other so-called "handcuff" knots, is really no such thing. It is far more likely to be tied as a make-&-mend suitcase handle or gift-package ornamentation, or (in rope) for civil engineering or salvage operations.

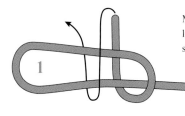

Make a bight in one end of a lanyard or lashing and wrap the end around it in a series of not less than three turns (1, 2).

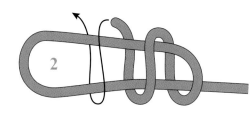

Then tuck a bight from the working end back through the turns, alongside the standing part of the line (3).

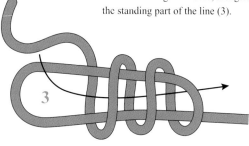

ORIGIN

This knot appeared in *The Ashley Book of Knots* (originally published in New York in 1944) by Clifford W. Ashley, who described it at that time as a "commercial cord curtain holdback."

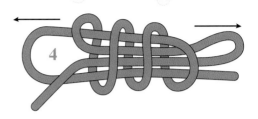

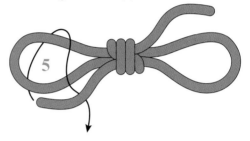

Pull the standing leg of both loops in opposite directions to tighten the knot (4).

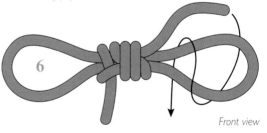

Adjust the loops to the required size and lock each in turn with a half hitch applied over its opposite number (5, 6).

*Front view*

Tighten the knot again (7).

*Rear view*

Today this knot has become a mere party-piece for
knot tyers keen to impress with their skill and dexterity.
It can also be used, however, to embellish the uniforms of
bandsmen and women, or as a central motif in appliqué
pictures and embroidery; or even as an improvised
hackamore or rope bridle for horse, mule, camel, or
other saddled creature.

Form three underhand loops,
one after the other, and overlap
them as shown (1, 2).

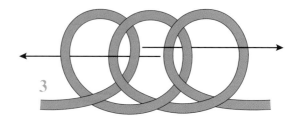

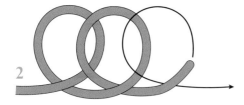

## ORIGIN

A "jury mast" was a temporary or
occasional mast on a newly launched
ship that did not yet have its permanent
masts and spars; it could also serve in
the short term in place of a mast that
had been carried away in a storm, battle,
or some other extraordinary event.

Pull the right-hand edge of the left-
hand loop to the right, going over,
under, over; at the same time, pull the
left-hand edge of the right-hand loop
to the left, going under, over, under (3).

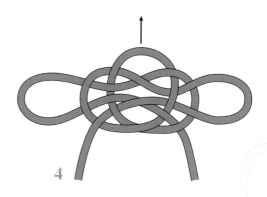

4

Obtain the necessary slack to pull out the middle loop (4, 5). Insert whatever is to be seized, through the central space marked X.

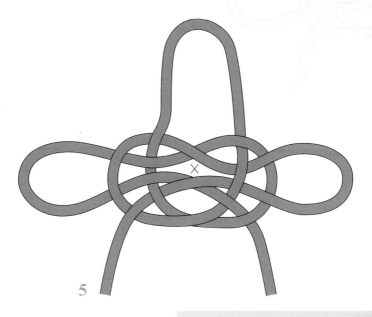

5

The jury mast knot was a rigger's expedient—an interwoven bracelet to whose loops and ends could be attached the necessary stays in order to raise and hold such a mast upright.

# TURK'S HEAD
## 2L x 5B

This unassuming relative of the diverse Turk's head family (*see also pages 86–91*) deserves to be better known. Use it in cord or thong as ornamentation for fancy knotting or braided leather work. Tie it around trashcans and plant pots. Wear it as a bracelet, anklet, or finger ring.

**1**

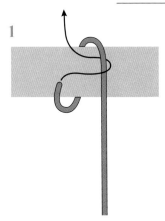

Tie a half-knot around the chosen item, starting to the left of the standing part (in the example shown), then tuck the working end a second time (1, 2).

**2**

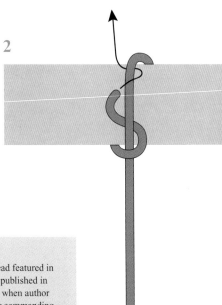

ORIGIN
This least-known Turk's head featured in *The Bushcraft Handbooks* published in 1952 in Sydney, Australia, when author Richard H. Graves (former commanding officer of the Australian Jungle Survival & Rescue Detachment) recommended it for binding the ends of hunting crops.

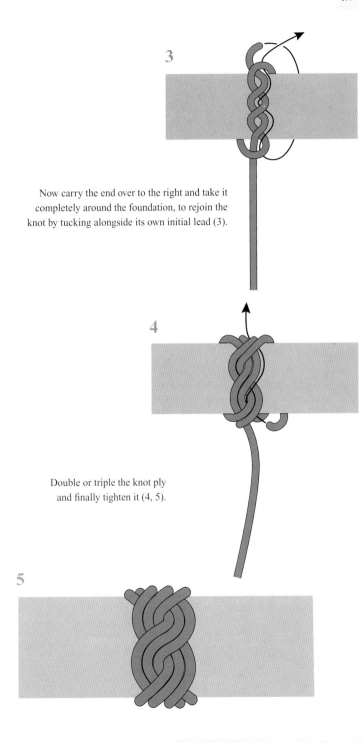

**3**

Now carry the end over to the right and take it completely around the foundation, to rejoin the knot by tucking alongside its own initial lead (3).

**4**

Double or triple the knot ply and finally tighten it (4, 5).

**5**

# PRUSIK BOTTLE SLING

Carrying liquids in jugs, jars, bottles, and carboys can be an awkward and arduous task. A sling lashed around the neck of any such container, with loops that act as carrying handles, is a labor- (and back-) saving trick.

**1**

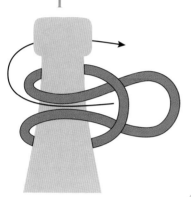

Tie a basic bale, sling, or ring hitch (1) in a knotted or endless sling or strop around the neck of the container to be carried.

**2**

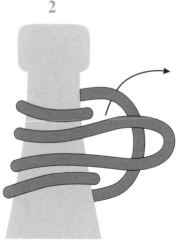

## ORIGIN

The ancient Greeks and Romans used jar slings to manhandle their amphorae. Austrian professor of music Dr. Karl Prusik invented the knot that bears his name in World War One; in 1931, he published instructions on using it as a means of self-rescue ascent for climbers.

Take the retaining bight around a second time and retuck it (2, 3). What results is the classic double Prusik knot used by climbers as a slide-&-grip knot.

**3**

Pull out the bight closest to the container once more, insert a half twist (4), and tuck the other bight through it (5). Tighten all of the turns, then tighten them again, before use.

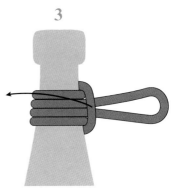

**4**

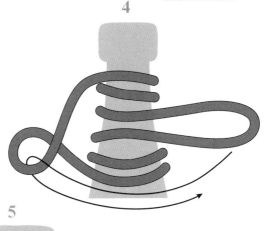

**5**

However, this adaptation as a bottle sling was dreamed up by Dr. Harry Asher of Birmingham, England, and first appeared in his *A New System of Knotting* (1986).

# Indian jug handle

This knot has also been described as an Indian bridle knot, and is similar to hackamore knots (such as the Fiador or Theodore, *see pages 108–109)* that were used by Western American frontiersmen and women. See pages 178–179 for a brief outline of why and how jug, jar, or bottle slings can be usefully employed.

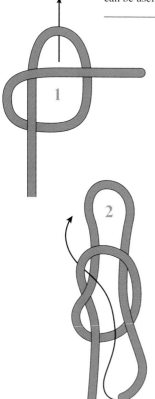

Form an uncompleted overhand knot, then pull a bight through the loop to create a simple noose (1, 2).

Tuck the working end up through the pair of entwined knot parts, as shown (3), then take the end around behind the upper bight and tuck it down, from front to back, through its own bight.

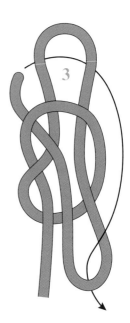

ORIGIN
Dr. Robert M. Wolfe, M.D., of Chicago discovered the way of tying this knot that is illustrated here and let it be known in *Knotting Matters* issue no. 55 (March 1997), although the knot itself features in earlier mid-20th century knotting manuals as an Indian bridle knot.

Arrange the completed knot into a
bracelet with one loop and two
loose ends (4), then insert the neck
of whatever is to be seized and carried
into the central knot space marked X.

Tie the two ends together, having first inserted
the longer one through the loop, to create a
couple of self-equalizing handles (5).

# LAPP-TO-STRAP

Wilderness pioneers, whether hauling sleds on Arctic expeditions or mending the worn harness of pack animals, as well as stay-at-home hobbyists of every kind, could usefully employ this simple method of joining a cord or rope to a leather or webbing strap.

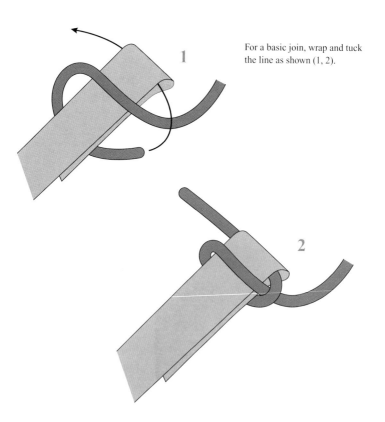

For a basic join, wrap and tuck the line as shown (1, 2).

## ORIGIN

The Lapp knot tied as a joining knot in two lengths of rope or cord (*see page 76*) superficially resembles a sheet bend (and is sometimes called a "false" sheet bend). This hybrid Lapp-to-strap was recommended in *Knotting Matters* issue no. 52 (April 1996) by Robert Pont.

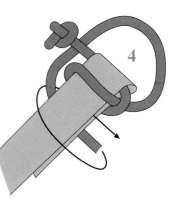

**3**

Add an overhand stopper knot for added security (3).

To create an optional extra loop, bring the running end around to the opposite side of the strap and repeat the tying process (4, 5).

**4**

**5**

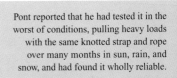

Pont reported that he had tested it in the worst of conditions, pulling heavy loads with the same knotted strap and rope over many months in sun, rain, and snow, and had found it wholly reliable.

# FALMOUTH CARRICK BEND

There are several carrick bends which, with their simple forms (compared to some knots) and concentrated nip, are suitable for joining cables and other ropes of large diameter, although they work well in smaller cordage too.

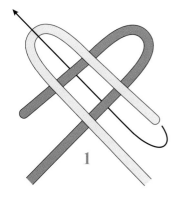

Form a bight in the end of each line and lay one on top of the other, as shown (1).

Take the end that lies on top down and around beneath its companion bight, then tuck it up through itself (2).

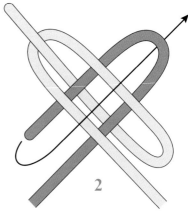

ORIGIN

This easy tying method was described and illustrated by Englishman Owen K. Nuttall of Huddersfield, England, in *Knotting Matters* issue no. 23 (April 1988).

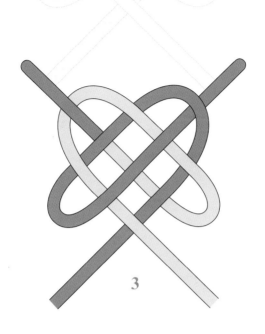

3

Similarly, take the end that lies
underneath over the top of the
developing knot and tuck it
down through its own bight (3).

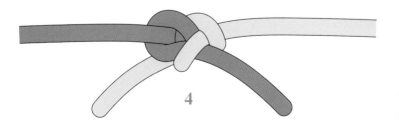

4

Pull both standing parts in opposite
directions, then let the knot capsize
into its final form (4).

# OPEN SESAME BEND

Here is another of those bends that consist of two interlocked overhand knots. It is a strong and secure specimen, which has the added advantage that tugging upon both short ends partially opens up the knot—hence its name—making it easier to untie.

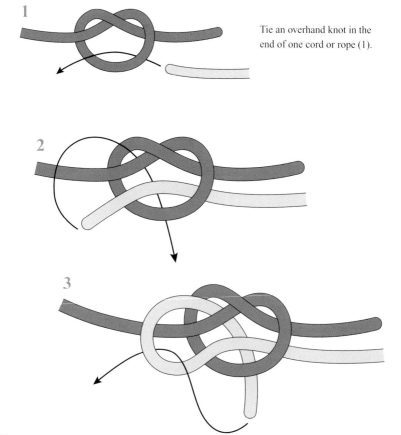

Tie an overhand knot in the end of one cord or rope (1).

Insert the other end through the mouth or belly of the initial knot, then tuck and tie it as shown (2, 3, 4).

## ORIGIN

Dr. Harry Asher discovered this knot, which he described in *Knotting Matters* issue no. 43 (April 1993). The name is a direct reference to the charmed words by which the door of the robber's dungeon flew open in the *Arabian Nights* tale of the Forty Thieves.

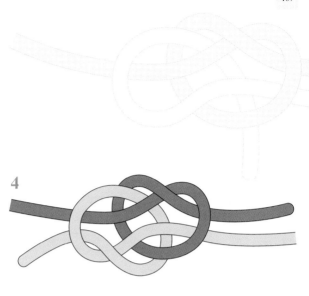

**4**

**5**

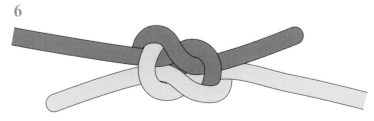

Tighten the knot by pulling on
both standing parts (5, 6).

**6**

# COLLARED HITCH

This robust holdfast will withstand a steady or intermittent load from various directions, and may even cope with a longitudinal pull.

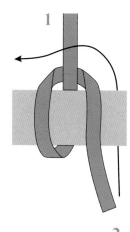

Lead the end around the foundation and behind its own standing part to create a sort of jacket collar (1).

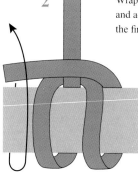

Wrap again, in the opposite direction, and add a second collar opposing the first one (2, 3).

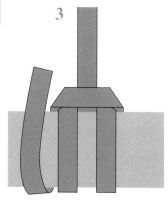

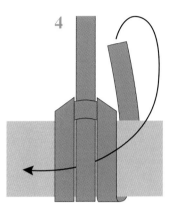

**4**

Now turn the work around, before bring the working end over, from back to front, and inserting a locking tuck that goes over one, under one, over one (4).

*Rear view*

Methodically work the knot tight (5).

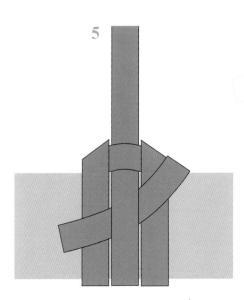

**5**

# PIWICH KNOT

This reinforced version of a bale, ring, sling, or hook hitch is less likely to fall apart when the strain imposed by the load slackens temporarily, and may also be slightly stronger. There are two methods of tying it: when tied with an end, that end ought then to be knotted to the standing part of the webbing for complete security; when working with a preformed loop, strop, or sling, tying this knot in the bight is the only available option.

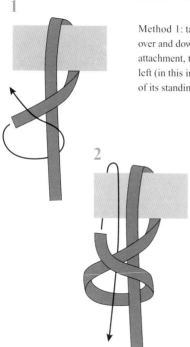

**1**

Method 1: take the working end over and down behind the point of attachment, then bring it from right to left (in this instance) across the front of its standing part (1).

**2**

Take a turn with the end around the standing part, before going behind, over, and down the front of the point of attachment once more. Then tuck the working end through the loop beside its original lead (2) and tighten (3).

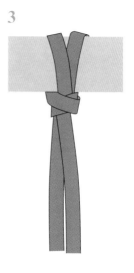

**3**

ORIGIN

This knot was reported in *Knotting Matters* issue no. 47 (December 1994) by Robert Pont of France, who first spotted it in Quebec and kindly named it the Piwich knot after the child whom he witnessed tying it (Piwich Kust, of the Bois Brule tribe).

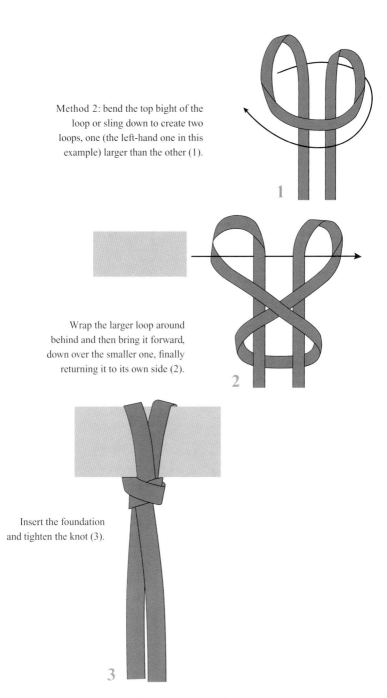

Method 2: bend the top bight of the loop or sling down to create two loops, one (the left-hand one in this example) larger than the other (1).

Wrap the larger loop around behind and then bring it forward, down over the smaller one, finally returning it to its own side (2).

Insert the foundation and tighten the knot (3).

# CHAIN STITCH LASHING

There is a continual need, whether aboard a smart sailboat
or tidying one's garden shed, garage, or closets, to lash
together assorted items. This could take the form of
furling unused sails in port or wrapping a rolled carpet for
transportation. The chain stitch lashing will do the job, yet
it may be cast off by pulling on one end, when it comes
undone faster than a zipper.

---

**1**

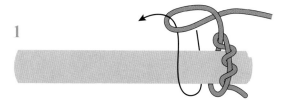

Start with a timber hitch (*see page
58*) and proceed with the long
working end to make a bight (1).

**2**

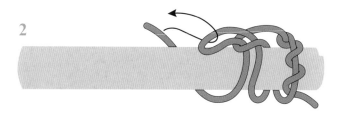

Take the end around whatever is
to be lashed and insert a second
bight through the first one (2).

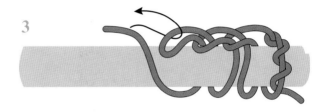

**3**

Repeat the process as often as required by the length of both package and available cord (3).

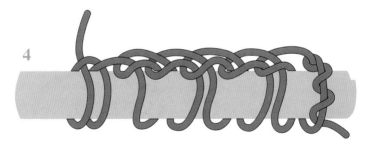

**4**

Finish off with at least two half hitches (you can add one or two more to be sure) (4).

# VERSATACKLE

Few households possess a proper rope-rigged block-&-tackle, but this cleverly improvised alternative will apply (and multiply) tension wherever it is required. Tie it in small cord to clamp new picture frames, chairs, or other woodwork while the glue dries; use it to hoist heavy loads or haul out a mired-in vehicle; tighten guylines and other standing rigging on tent, flagpole, or mast. It really is a versatile tackle.

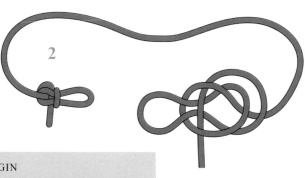

In one end of a long line tie a fixed-loop knot: the angler's loop (*see pages 68–69*) is ideal (1). Then, at a distance somewhat more than that of the points to be constrained by this tackle, tie a second angler's loop, so that the running end emerges from the side of the knot (2).

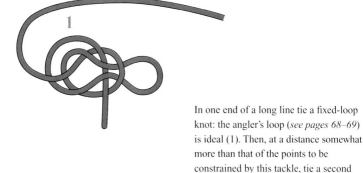

ORIGIN
This remarkable cordage contrivance first appeared in *Knotting Matters* issue no. 13 (October 1985), where it was described and illustrated by its inventor George Aldridge of south London, England.

Now pass one end through the first loop, back through the second, through the first loop again, and so on several times (3, 4, 5). Pull on the running end to exert a shortening force that brings the two loops closer together. Let go and it holds firm (although, for safety's sake, add a retaining half hitch or two). To release it, take out a turn or two from the loops, and loosen the entire arrangement.

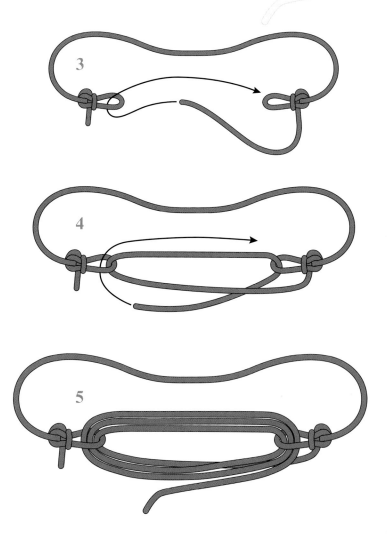

# BRAIDED
## INTERLOCKED LOOPS

Loops simply interlocked can in time weaken and even saw through one another. This arrangement spreads and minimizes abrasion, a function that can be invaluable in rope, cord, or small stuff such as fishing line, as well as to its user's peace of mind (and wallet or purse).

Tie a fixed loop (in this instance, a figure-eight loop, *see pages 166–167*) in the end of one of the lines to be joined and twist three loops into it (1, 2).

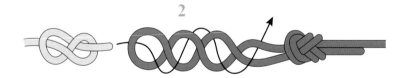

ORIGIN
This idea appeared in *The Hamlyn Book of Fishing Knots* by Geoffrey Budworth, published in 1999, and may have been his own invention.

Tie a loose figure-eight knot in the other line, and then weave the free or running end up and back through the other line's loop, precisely as shown, to create what is in effect a round four-strand plait or braid, like an old-fashioned telephone cord (3).

3

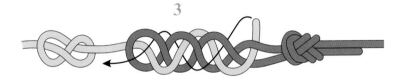

Complete the second figure-eight loop and tighten the knot (4).

4

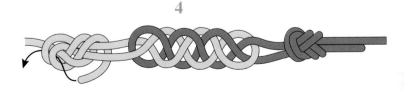

# BRAIDED LOOP

This elaborate fixed loop is a strong knot that, because of its interwoven form, has an inherent elasticity which absorbs some of the energy imposed by a shock loading, and thus increases the ultimate breaking strength of the line in which it is tied.

Arrange the line as shown, then commence a three-strand "pigtail" plait: bring the left-hand strand over to replace the center one (1), then the right-hand strand over to replace the center one (2), the left-hand strand over to replace the center one (3), and so on.

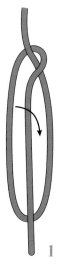

1

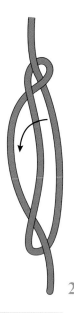

2

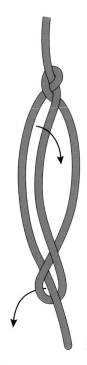

3

ORIGIN

This knot, called the Australian plait, appeared in *Practical Fishing Knots* (1991) by American writers Lefty Kreh and Mark Sosin.

Repeat the process until the lower
bight is only a little larger than the
size of the required loop, then double
the free or running end (4).

Wrap four or five turns around both bight
legs, as shown, then pull on the end to
eliminate the remaining small loop and
tighten the seizing that has resulted (5, 6.)

# Braided splice

This is a strong way to join two small lines—such as fishing lines—and, as with the previous knotted loop, the interwoven nature of the splice yields a degree of stretch that will absorb at least some of the energy of a shock loading, increasing the ultimate breaking strength.

Arrange the two ends of line to be joined as shown (1), then begin a three-strand "pigtail" braid (2, 3) (*see pages 198–199*).

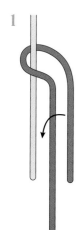

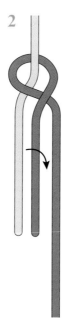

## ORIGIN

This splice was featured in the *Complete Book of Fishing Knots & Rigs* by Geoff Wilson, published by the Australian Fishing Network in 1995.

As the working ends of both lines shorten, double the one that began as a collar around the other one into a bight (4). Continue to plait, treating the bight as if it were a single line, but imparting a half-twist for added neatness each time the bight appears as an outside strand.

When the bight is used up, tuck the other working end down through it (5) and trim both ends close to the completed splice (6).

# FURTHER READING

From the hundreds of mainstream books and booklets about knotting that have been written since the beginning of the twentieth century, only a limited selection of those describing basic knotting has been listed below. These include a few climbing and fishing knot publications, for each of those pursuits enjoys a large following, but specialized topics—such as mathematical knot theory, the forensic analysis of knots and ligatures, rope splicing, netting, rigging, conjurors' rope tricks, and macramé and other decorative knotting (for example, tying friendship braids and Chinese knotting)—are not included.

Retail book stores either stock or can order many publications (including old titles, if they have been reprinted in an up-to-date format), although some will inevitably be out-of-print and must be searched for in secondhand bookstores or at garage sales.

Adkins, Jan, *String—Tying it Up, Tying it Down*, 1992, ISBN 0-68418875-9

Asher, Harry, *The Alternative Knot Book*, 1989, ISBN 0-7136-5950-5

Ashley, Clifford W., *The Ashley Book of Knots*, 1944, ISBN 0-57109659-X

Berthier, Marc P.G., *The Art of Knots*, English translation 1977,
ISBN 0-356-08150-8

Bigon, Mario, & Regazzoni, Guido, *The Century Guide to Knots*, 1981,
ISBN 0-7126-0089-2

Blandford, Percy W., *Practical Knots & Ropework*, 1980,
ISBN 0-1806-9956-2

Bounford, Trevor, *Knots*, 2001, ISBN 0-00-710151-1

Budworth, Geoffrey, *The Ultimate Encyclopedia of Knots & Ropework*,
2000, ISBN 1-84309-138-0

Fink, Thomas, & Mao, Yong, *The 85 Ways to Tie a Tie*, 1999,
ISBN 1-84115-249-8

Gerber, Ham, *Making Discoveries in Knots*, 1990, ISBN 0-8323-0475-1

Goodhind, Wendy, *The Girl Guide Association Knot Book*, 1998,
ISBN 0-85260-146-8

Graumont, Raoul, & Hensel, John, *Encyclopedia of Knots and Fancy Rope
Work*, 4th edition 1952, no ISBN

Herzog, Bill, *Tying Strong Fishing Knots*, 1995, ISBN 1-57188-022-4

Hin, Floris, *The Colour Book of Knots*, 1982, ISBN 0-333-34164-3

Judkins, Steve, & Davison, Tim, *Knots & Splices*, 1998,
ISBN 1-8986-6-0476

MacNally, Bob, *Fishermen's Knots, Fishing Rigs, and How to Use Them*,
1993, ISBN 0-9646265-1-9

Miles, Roger, *Symmetric Bends—How to Join Two Lengths of Cord*, 1995,
ISBN 981-02-2194-0

Newman, Bob, & Knight, Tami, *Knots around the Home*, 1997,
ISBN 0-89732-207-X

Noonan, Michael, *Climbing Knots—for Lefties and Righties*, 1997,
ISBN 1-57034-053-6

Notley, Larry V., *Fly Leaders & Knots*, 1998, ISBN 1-57188-122-2

Pawson, Des, *Pocket Guide to Knots & Splices*, 2001, ISBN 1-85648-604-4

Raleigh, Duane, *Knots & Ropes for Climbers*, 1998, ISBN 0-8117-2871-4

Rosenow, Frank, *Seagoing Knots*, 1990, ISBN 0-393-03338-4

Sosin, Mark, & Kreh, Lefty, *Practical Fishing Knots*, 1991,
ISBN 0-71346993-5

Taylor, Roger C., *Knowing the Ropes*, 1989, ISBN 0-87742-970-7

Toss, Brion, *Knots*, 1990, ISBN 0-688-09415-5

Trower, Nola, *Knots and Ropework*, 1992, ISBN 1-85223-705-8

Warner, Charles, *A Fresh Approach to Knotting & Ropework*, 1992,
ISBN 0-959203-3-X

# USEFUL INFORMATION AND WEBSITES

International Guild of Knot Tyers (IGKT)

The IGKT was established in 1982 and its membership is now approaching 1,500. It is a UK-registered educational charity, but has a worldwide membership and is strongly represented in the United States. Members keep in touch by means of a members' handbook and a quarterly magazine, *Knotting Matters,* which contains informed articles, expert tips, letters, editorial comment, and news and views about everything to do with knots. In the UK, IGKT members enjoy two major gatherings each year, but local groups (both in the UK and other territories) meet more frequently for lectures, demonstrations, and workshops. For further details (including subscription fees and an application form) contact Nigel Harding (IGKT Honorary Secretary) at: 16 Egles Grove, Uckfield, East Sussex, TN22 2BY, England. Tel: +44 (0)1825 760425; e-mail: igkt@nigelharding.demon.co.uk

IGKT websites

International Guild of Knot Tyers: www.igkt.craft.org
IGKT, North American branch: http://www.igktnab.org/
IGKT, Pacific American branch: http://www.pab.org/
IGKT, Texas branch: http://www.texasknot.tripod.com/

## Animated knot-tying

Boatsafe, Stuart, Florida: www.boatsafe.com/kids/knots/htm

Boy Scout Troop 9, Billings, Montana: www.troop9.org/knots

Folsom's Knots and Knotting Page: http://www.folsoms.net/knots/

42 Brighton Scout Group, East Sussex, England:
www.mistral.co.uk/42brghtn/knots

## Knot-tying and knotting links

Folsom's Knots and Knotting Page (50 useful knots, including some
animated ones, plus links and knot books, from Alan Folsom):
http://www.folsoms.net/knots/

Knots (knots for Scouts, with an index of about 130 common knots):
http://www.scoutingresources.org.uk/knots_index.html

Martin Combs (knot links and resources):
http://members.tripod.com/~knots/index-2.html

NetKnots.com (knots for camping, fishing, and boating):
http://www.netknots.com

Peter Suber (comprehensive coverage and links under three main headings:
knot tying, knot theory, and knot art):
http://www.earlham.edu/~peters/knotlink.htm

Ropers Knots Page (links to knot sites and an in-depth index of knots on
the Web): http://www.realknots.com

Scout Association of Australia (index of knots and lashings):
http://www.scouts.asn.au/knot_idx.html

## Rope manufacturers and stockists

Brion Toss (American sailboat rigger and knotting writer):
http://briontoss.com

Jimmy Green Marine (UK chandler stocking ropes, rigging, and safety
equipment): www.jimmygreen.co.uk

KJK Ropeworks (UK manufacturers of rope products and suppliers of
cords and fittings): www.kjkropeworks.co.uk

Liros Ropes Ltd (German manufacturer of synthetic and natural fibers for
yachting purposes): http://www.liros.com

Marlow Ropes Ltd (a leading manufacturer in the UK of sailboat ropes and
cordage): www.marlowropes.com

Rock-n-Rescue (Pennsylvania-based company supplying climbers, cavers,
and rope-rescue teams): http://www.rocknrescue.com

Samson Rope Technologies (US rope manufacturer):
http://www.samsonrope/com

U-Braid-It Braiding Supply Co. (New Mexico mail-order suppliers of
braiding materials for horse tack): http://www.ubraidit.com

# INDEX

# Acknowledgments

The author freely acknowledges the influence of all those earlier writers, illustrators, and publishers who—through their numerous and varied books, booklets, and technical manuals—taught him much of what he understands about knots. A great deal of their knotting knowhow reappears in this book, although considerable effort has been made to give a personal and, wherever possible, original presentation and spin to the data. Any preferences and prejudices that may be apparent in the contents (whether inspired or misguided) are the author's alone.

A special note of thanks goes to his editor Mandy Greenfield and illustrator John Fowler who, as key players in the Ivy Press's production team, were able, in mere months, to display a competence with the portrayal of knots that had taken him years to acquire.